The Aryan: Recasting Constructs

The Aryan

Recasting Constructs

Romila Thapar

Three Essays
COLLECTIVE

Second Reprint January 2011
First Edition June 2008

ISBN 978-81-88789-68-9

Three Essays Collective
B-957 Palam Vihar, GURGAON (Haryana) 122 017 India
Phone: 91-124 2369023, +91 98681 26587, +91 98683 44843
info@threeessays.com Website: www.threeessays.com
Printed and bound by Glorious Printers, New Delhi

For Shirish and Rajani
... as always ...

Acknowledgements

The essays in this collection have been previously published and are being reproduced here either in full or in extract and with some editing. Their locations in the original publications are listed below.

1. The Historiography of the Concept of 'Aryan' [Romila Thapar et al. (eds.), *India: Historical Beginnings and the Concept of the Aryan*, NBT, New Delhi 2006, pp. 1–40]
2. Some Appropriations of the Theory of Aryan Race and the Beginnings of Indian History [Daud Ali (ed.), *Invoking the Past*, OUP, Delhi 1999, pp. 15–35]
3. Exploring Societies of the Early Past [*Proceedings of the Indian History Congress*, Delhi 1970, pp. 15–39, xxxi Session, Varanasi 1969, Presidential Address, Ancient Indian History]
4. The *Ṛgveda*: Encapsulating Social Change [K.N.Panikkar et al., (eds.), *The Making of History*, Tulika, Delhi 2000, pp. 11–40]
5. The Archaeological Background to the *Agnicayana* Ritual [F.Staal (ed.), *Agni*, 2 vols., Berkeley 1983, vol. II, pp. 1–40]

Every effort has been made to contact copyright holders. The publishers shall be happy to make good in future editions any errors or omissions brought to their attention.

Contents

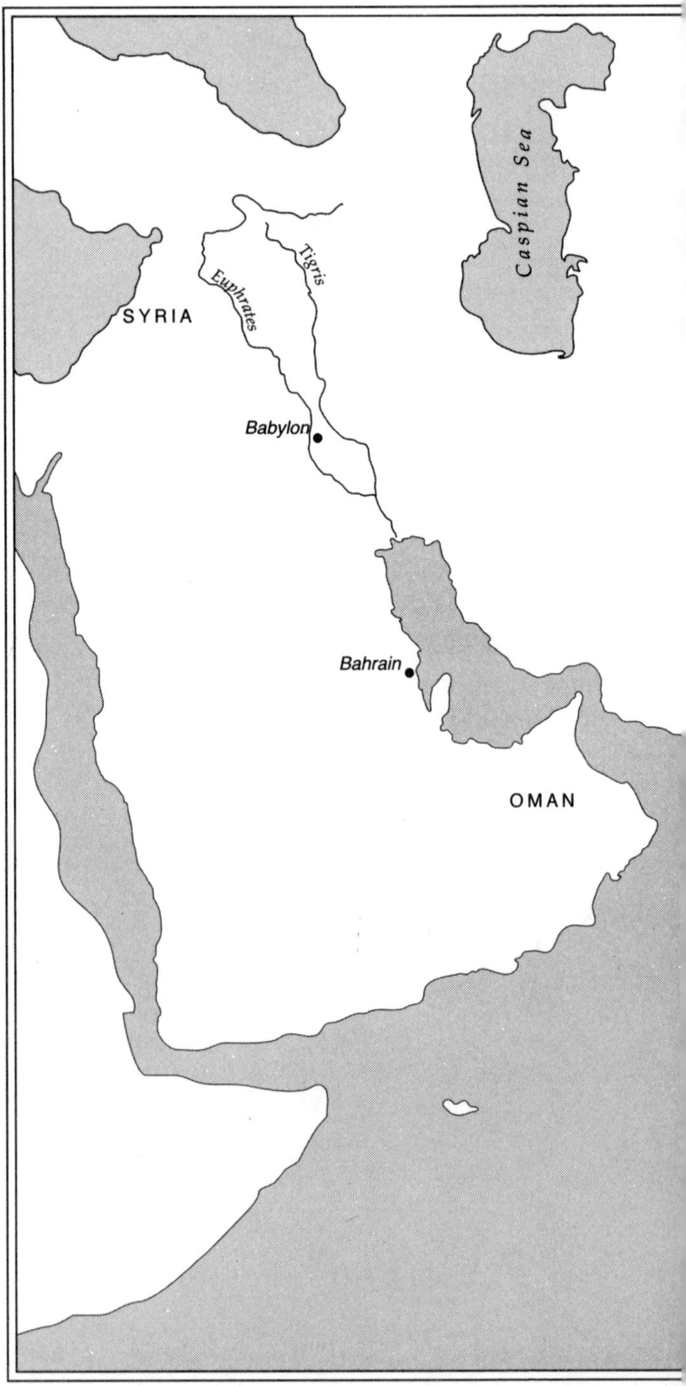
Caspian Sea
Tigris
Euphrates
SYRIA
Babylon
Bahrain
OMAN

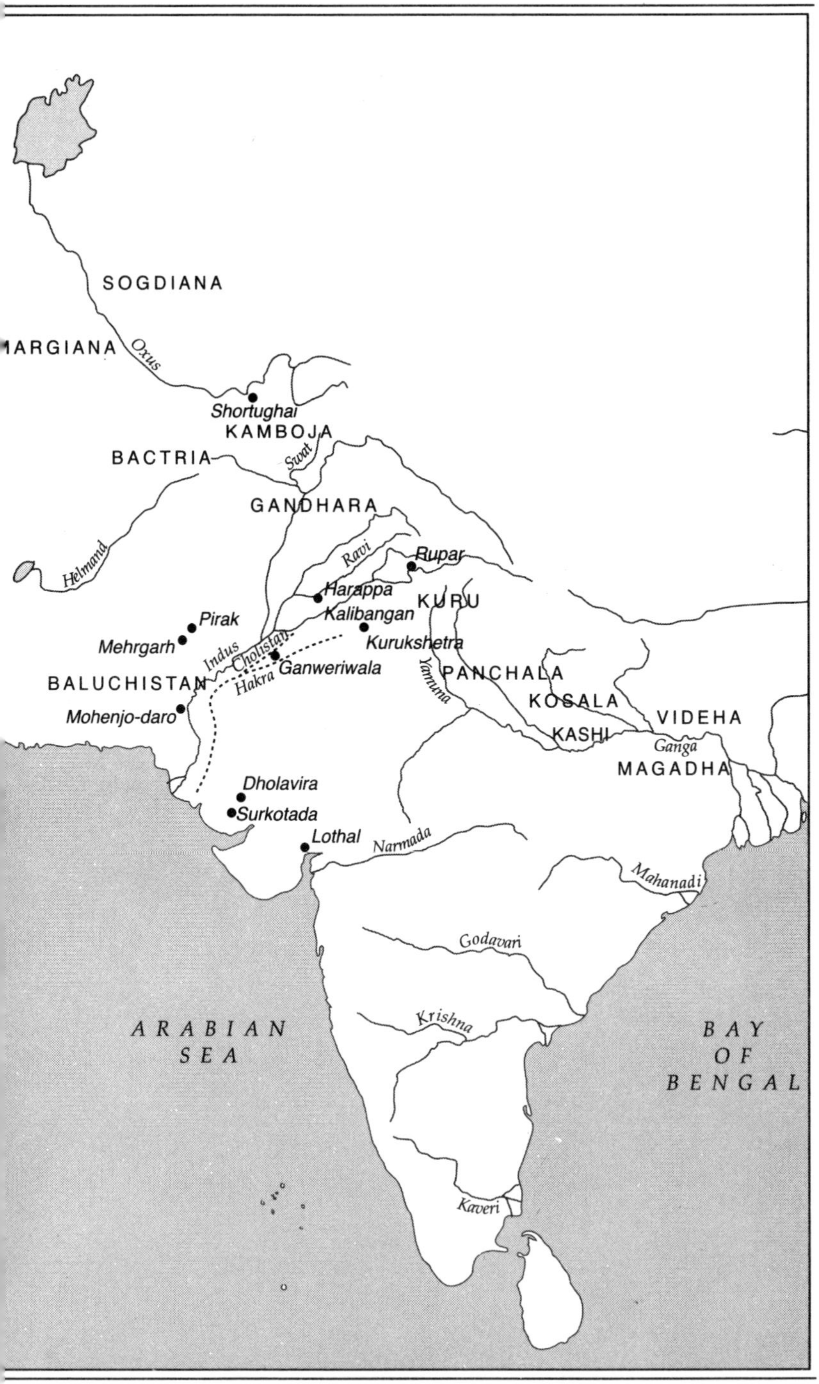
SOGDIANA
MARGIANA
Oxus
Shortughai
KAMBOJA
BACTRIA
Swat
GANDHARA
Helmand
Ravi
Rupar
Harappa
KURU
Pirak
Kalibangan
Mehrgarh
Kurukshetra
Indus
Cholistan
Ganweriwala
BALUCHISTAN
Hakra
Yamuna
PANCHALA
KOSALA
Mohenjo-daro
VIDEHA
KASHI
Ganga
MAGADHA
Dholavira
Surkotada
Lothal
Narmada
Mahanadi
Godavari
Krishna
ARABIAN SEA
BAY OF BENGAL
Kaveri

Preface

To identify the Aryan is to search for that which remains elusive. There have been many definitions based on multiple and diverse factors and there are therefore inevitable disagreements about both the identification and the meaning of the concept. Some of the discussion focuses on specific evidence but broader questions follow from the constructs: the ideas and theories that emerge from the synthesizing of facts, from analyses and from what is presented as a concept. It is therefore helpful to know what these ideas and theories are, how they took shape and what influence they have had or may continue to have on historical interpretation. Varying agencies change the evolving of constructs, which in the process, are recast by those interpreting the evidence. These essays are implicitly a comment on such recasting pertaining to what has generally been referred to as 'the Aryans'.

These constructs draw upon evidence and inference in diverse ways. Assessing the validity of a definition requires evaluating the reliability of the evidence and the logic of the reasoning in its presentation. A few of the more plausible ones are discussed here and others are implied. It is helpful to keep in mind that the study of the Aryan is as yet not an area of universal certainties, although some preconditions can be taken as given.

I am aware of the long span of time between the earliest and the last of the essays. In the absence of startlingly new discoveries relating to the period of the two millennia (c. 2600–600 BC) that have been brought into the discussion through diverse theories, variations of interpretation have largely focused on ways of reading the existing data. There are bound to be repetitions in this collection since the essays were written for varying occasions. These I have not deleted since such passages are integral to the argument. Besides, repetitions become a form of emphasis.

This collection of essays is not intended as a definitive statement on the subject. Definitive statements about the remote past are inevitably somewhat tentative since they have to contend with some degree of speculation. My intention has been to explore attempted definitions and reconstructions in the light of complex evidence, and going beyond that, to suggest further explorations.

New Delhi
March 2008

Romila Thapar

Abbreviations

ṚV	*Ṛgveda*
SV	*Sāmaveda*
YV	*Yajurveda*
AV	*Atharvaveda*
ŚB/Śat. Brāh.	*Śatapatha Brāhmaṇa*
TS	*Taittirīya Saṃhitā*
VS	*Vājasaneyi Saṃhitā*
MS	*Maitrāyaṇī Saṃhitā*
AŚS	*Āśvalāyana Śrautasūtra*
BŚS	*Baudhāyana Śrautasūtra*
KŚS	*Kātyāyana Śrautasūtra*
MB	*Mahābhārata*
Ram	*Rāmāyaṇa*

INTRODUCTION

I

In the last couple of decades there has been a revival of interest in what are popularly called 'the Aryans'. The meaning of the term in the public mind remains a bit vague and arbitrarily conflates race, ethnicity, culture, language, religion and geography – some of which are now discarded elements and others although essential to the argument cannot be indiscriminately brought into play. This is more so where past histories are being related to current identities. The study of the Aryans has been a contentious historical subject used as it has been – and continues to be – in various ways to suit a variety of ideologies.

What is sometimes called 'the Aryan Problem' is not a simple problem of putting together the evidence for a historical period with easy answers. It is probably the most complex question in early Indian history and it requires considerable expertise in the interpretation of the evidence which ranges from ecology to philology. The basic expertise requires some familiarity with at least four fields of enquiry: historiography, archaeology, linguistics and social anthropology. The evidence from these when inter-related provides historical hypotheses. Historians today map cultures, observe their varied inter-connections at different levels of society and try to understand the societies that emerge. That there is continual fresh evidence from archaeology and linguistics further complicates the analyses.

Historiography has now become preliminary to most historical studies as it introduces the intellectual context which shapes historical generalizations. It relates to the concepts with which historians work, their ideological roots and their role in explaining and understanding the past. This is particularly significant when a subject is controversial and where ideological concerns can colour a reading of the evidence.

The discussion of the Aryan in India is an appropriate example. There was a time when race was a primary consideration in defining 'the Aryan'. Now language is important to the definition. For some the focus has shifted to whether the Aryans were alien or indigenous. Many scholars prefer to focus on the more relevant question of what is meant by Aryan rather than who were 'the Aryans'. This involves analyzing whether it was a kind of cultural package that was imposed on an existing population when those that brought it settled amidst them, and this monolith then became foundational to Indian civilization; or, whether cultural elements came in with small circuits of migrants who settled amidst other cultures and new cultural forms gradually evolved. The evidence is substantially of two kinds: archaeological and linguistic.

Archaeological data for this period and subject is extensive. It involves an awareness of Harappan and post-Harappan cultures especially those of the Punjab and the Doāb, the Indo-Iranian borderlands, the Oxus valley and north-eastern Iran. Coping with fresh evidence from such a large area makes further demands on organizing the argument. The earlier approach of selecting an item from an excavation and trying to identify it with an object mentioned in literary sources is no longer feasible. Comparisons between societies as a whole are more valid when seen as systems rather than as individual artifacts. This involves juxtaposing a combination of items that go into the making of a culture whether they come from archaeology or from a text. Thus where a cluster of items are mentioned in the *Ṛgveda* such as horses, chariots, cattle-herding and the rituals of sacrifice, the archaeological counterpart of such a cluster is sought from the excavations of specific cultures. Such artifacts are not just items in a list of material goods; they provide clues to the structure of the society that they refer to.

Much the same applies to the method of linguistics. In terms of nineteenth century philology it was possible to suggest connections and language identities by resort to similarities in words from two different languages. But the discipline of linguistics requires that the word be placed in the larger syntactic context and similarity in the context is essential. This is particularly important for example, when attempts are being made to decipher the Indus script by applying known languages. Linguistic evidence for this period comes from the Indo-Aryan of the Vedic corpus and its earliest composition, the *Ṛgveda*. But it also requires an awareness of the other languages in its neighbourhood such as Dravidian and Austro-Asiatic or Munda. Comparative data for Indo-Aryan is available in the Iranian *Avesta* and from scattered fragments of Proto Indo-Aryan in Anatolia. Familiarity with the linguistic evidence is again quite demanding. In addition there has to be an understanding of the contents of texts, keeping in mind that Vedic Sanskrit is a specialized form of Sanskrit and not every Sanskritist has expertise in it.

Social anthropology is a more recent addition to the agenda of both the archaeologist and the historian. It provides some direction in using a comparative analysis to explain how societies of various kinds function. The idea is not just to import a model from anthropology or from ethno-archaeology and apply it to the data, but to enquire into the type of questions that social anthropologists ask of various categories of pre-modern societies, and then ask similar questions where feasible, of the archaeological and historical data. Let me in passing mention one interesting comparison of this sort. The anthropologist Evans-Pritchard worked on the Nuer society, a cattle keeping society of Sudan.[1] Bruce Lincoln made a comparative study of this material with the data from the *Ṛgveda* and the *Avesta*, all cattle-keeping societies.[2] It has been the subject of contention but the discussion has resulted in some useful insights into the functioning of such societies. This was also what D. D. Kosambi emphasised in the concept of a living prehistory in India – that there are earlier social forms existing in the rural areas and historians should study these.[3]

In discussing the notion of the Aryan, a fundamental question relates to the spread of the Indo-Aryan language. How does a language spread among people who are speaking other languages at the same time? And together with the spread of a language there are many other items of culture that are also mutually appropriated. It was earlier argued that conquest and warfare brought about the acceptance of the language of the victorious by those conquered. But even where there were no large scale conquests languages are known to have gradually changed.

Historians look to factors such as a change in society and economy possibly accompanied by the introduction of new technologies, and the propagation of new rituals. The relevant questions then would be that given that the Ṛgvedic society was an agro-pastoral society how did it relate to similar local societies or to societies of cultivators? Were they all clan-based societies with chiefs as their authority in which case similarities made inter-relations easier? What was the social and economic impact of new technologies of transport and communication such as the horse, the chariot and the later use of iron artifacts as superior to copper-bronze. It becomes necessary to establish not only when such new technologies were introduced but how they altered society. Rituals can have a dramatic effect as doubtless the Vedic *yajña*s did in the ambience of what were rather small settlements of the time. Claims to magic and the supernatural would have furthered the effect.

Knowledge requires the teasing out of complexities and this cannot be done by insisting on the answer to a question being either this or that – what I like to call the one-bite answer that the media has now made so fashionable. Often, it is the nuances in between the options that push ideas forward and encourage explanations. My attempt therefore, is not to claim definitive answers but rather to lay out the field as it were, explain where we are at and indicate by implication the directions in which the analyses could proceed.

The essays included in this book were written during the last forty years and on various occasions. The arguments that I have been making are consistent since the evidence over the years has not been of a kind as to negate my initial argument in any major way. Some honing would of course be inevitable. The essays are an attempt to integrate the evidence rather than to keep it distinct since integration is of the essence in analyzing historical themes and more so this subject. There is bound to be some degree of overlap in the essays. I have not pruned this because in a sense repetition becomes a form of emphasis and there are aspects that I think need continual emphasis.

The first essay is historiographical and is an attempt to trace the history of the concept 'the Aryan': how it was introduced into the study of the beginnings of Indian history and how it has been used by scholars and non-scholars in the past two centuries. That the concept was constantly filtered through contemporary ideological demands becomes obvious. In the late eighteenth century attention was drawn to the possibility of monogenesis in relation to Sanskrit, Greek, Latin and other languages suggesting a common ancestry. In the nineteenth century this became a focus of some philological studies and was extended to other ideological concerns both in Europe and in India.

The second essay takes up a segment of this ideological function and examines it at greater length. A comparison is made between Phule's reading and the Hindutva reading to show how the same data was interpreted from two ideological positions. These and other readings in India were linked in part to the nationalist agenda and also, although to a lesser extent, to the politics of caste.

The third essay, written almost forty years ago, negates the idea of an Aryan invasion and attempts to co-relate archaeological and literary evidence to suggest small-scale migrations of Aryan speakers facilitating the innovation of cultural forms. These gave a structure to Indian society as is reflected in various facets of the Vedic corpus, different from the predominant forms of Harappan society. I have included this early essay in part to underline the fact that the questions that should be asked of our data have either not been asked or else not adequately answered. Part of the reason for this is that discussion has got diverted into the cul-de-sac of arguments about the indigenous or foreign identity of 'the Aryans'.

The fourth essay is an attempt to see the cultures as they evolved through a reading of the *Ṛgveda*, the earliest of the *Veda*s. The Vedic corpus in general and the *Ṛgveda* in particular, have been widely discussed as encapsulating religious ideas. But such texts, and especially the more successful ones, have throughout history also been reflections on and comments about, the societies from which they emanated. This aspect with regard to the Vedic corpus needs further attention.

The fifth essay continues this theme but is more specific in its analysis of the sacrificial ritual of the *agnicayana* of post-Ṛgvedic times. This is done from the perspective of cultural inter-relations juxtaposing archaeological data with literary descriptions. Looking at the material remains and objects of a culture that are available to us from archaeology and comparing them with textual descriptions also involves examining the process of how the object was made and comparing this with how its making is described in the text and what it symbolises. This can extend the meaning of an object and of its function.

II

Let me begin by setting out the space and time of the subject.

In terms of space we tend to think only of the geography of the Indian sub-continent and the boundaries of pre-partition India as they existed for British India. The focus is then narrowed down to north-western India.[4] But the geographical area of the archaeological and linguistic evidence is far more extensive. The links therefore are way beyond just the boundaries of India and involve some familiarity with more distant cultures.

In terms of archaeology the most extensive reach was that of the Harappa Culture or the Indus Civilization. From Shortughai in the Pamirs, evidence of Harappan settlements extends all the way down the Indus plain to the Arabian Sea, westwards into Baluchistan and Makran and touching the Indo-Iranian borderlands, and eastwards into Punjab and Haryana. More recently finds have been located in Oman in the Arabian peninsula particularly in the vicinity of copper mines. The Harappans were of course known to have trading relations with the Gulf and Mesopotamia. People of the ancient past did not confine themselves to one place. They travelled, migrated, traded and communicated across vast distances. This would probably have been too vast an area to host a single, unified culture. We have to consider the possibility of a multiplicity of cultures and societies, some fairly isolated and others in close contact but possibly functioning under a recognized and similar rubric.

Cultures of the post-Harappan period, some with occasional links have a more restricted geography. They extend only from the Indo-Iranian borderlands, across Punjab to the Doāb. In the north there are sites in the Swat valley. Some marginal links have been suggested between the Baluchistan borderlands and the Oxus valley. Sind and Gujarat subscribe to other cultures as do the sites of the Ganga plain although there is some overlap in the Doāb.

Varieties of Indo-Aryan and Indo-Iranian speakers can only be given an approximate geographical location which is not as firm as that of archaeological cultures. The geographical area of all these languages is extensive but not all are referred to in the same text and vary with the text. The geography takes a different direction from that of the Harappa Culture. Northern Syria and Anatolia is the location for Proto-Indo-Aryan, north-eastern Iran is the location for Old Iranian linked to the *Avesta*, and the speakers of Indo-Aryan as known from the *Ṛgveda* are restricted to the Indo-Iranian borderlands and Punjab up to the Doāb, which is geographically a small area. The history of Indo-Aryan has been extended backwards in time to the ancestral language of Indo-European and this brings in adjoining parts of central Asia. The presence of Indo-Aryan in the Ganga plain is attested to in the post-Ṛgvedic period.

Thus although the focus is often only on the Punjab we should not forget that there was also a large area of west Asia and of central Asia that had a bearing on this history, even if the Indo-Aryan of the *Ṛgveda* was not spoken in such a vast geographical area. The need for familiarity with the archaeology and linguistic history of other areas further complicates the problem. The geographical overlap between the Harappan sites and the place names associated with Indo-Aryan and Indo-Iranian is a limited area covering virtually only the Indo-Iranian borderlands and the Punjab. The thrust of the Harappan sites is southwards with maritime links whereas the Indo-Aryan speakers show up westwards and overland. The chronology of the two is also different.

The time bracket covers many centuries. There are some dates well-established among historians and archaeologists. The Harappan urban cultures referred to as the Mature Harappan, date from about 2600 to about 1700 BC, after which a decline in urbanism is apparent. The *Ṛgveda* is generally dated to the period after the decline of urbanism and would therefore date from about 1500 BC or a couple of centuries later. The subsequent *Veda*s – the *Sāma, Yajur* and *Atharva* – relating also to the Ganga plain are dated to the early first millennium BC.

However there are those who differ and would like to date the *Ṛgveda* to 3000 BC or even earlier and identify its culture with the Harappan cities, and who maintain that the Aryans are indigenous and there was therefore not even a migration of any kind let alone an invasion. To maintain this position it is even said that the *Ṛgveda* is prior to the Harappa Culture or that the authors of the Harappa Culture were Ṛgvedic Aryans. These views have become a matter of rather extensive controversy to say the least. This latter chronology, apart from not being able to muster firm evidence, creates huge problems for the historian. The discrepancy between Harappan urbanism and Ṛgvedic agro-pastoralism negates equivalence. Such an early chronology for the *Ṛgveda* is not supported by the linguistic evidence. It would for example, create a gap of at least 1500 years between the *Ṛgveda* and the other *Veda*s and therefore break what is known to be the continuity between the four *Veda*s. The insistence that the Aryans were a distinct people and that they were indigenous to the territory of British India is to impose present-day boundaries on the remote past which makes the statement anachronistic. Concepts such as 'indigenous' and 'alien' have to be precisely defined, which they are not in this case, and the definition has to conform to the time context for when it is being used. Needless to say identities are never permanent or static throughout history. They constantly change.

III

In order to understand how we have arrived at this point it might be useful to examine the emergence of the concept of 'the Aryan'. The beginnings of history as related in the *Purāṇa*s do not mention the Aryans as a category of people. *Ārya* is a status and is used for a variety of people. History starts with the genealogies of those referred to as *kṣatriya*s, defined as those who have *kṣatr* or power.

The *Purāṇa*s began to be composed in the early centuries AD and are therefore later than the *Ṛgveda* by almost fifteen hundred years. When scholars in the nineteenth century were reconstructing the history of India they argued that the *Veda*s were the earliest textual sources and their evidence should be used for the beginnings of Indian history. The *Ṛgveda* refers to *āryas* and *dāsa*s as distinct categories of people and the hymns are composed from the perspective of the *ārya*s. The word *varṇa* is associated with these categories. Its literal meaning is colour and since the *dāsa*s were associated with darkness the word was taken as a reference to race. However, the analogy of colour is often used for classifying differences and need not be taken literally.

The relationship between *ārya*s and *dāsa*s was frequently hostile. Physical differences are noticed but these are not given a racial connotation since there was no notion of race at that time. The language of the *dāsa*s was different and there are references to *mṛdhra vāc*, incorrect or hostile speech. The *dāsa*s are said to be phallus worshippers, *śiśnadeva,* and presumably because their rituals are different they are said to be *avrata*, without the recognized observances. The *dāsa*s are described as wealthy but niggardly and because they hide their wealth they are raided.

Prior to these studies there had been philological analyses of Sanskrit as a language and it was found to be similar to Greek and Latin and a few other European languages. It was argued that they all had a common ancestor and this was the hypothetical idea of monogenesis put forward by William Jones. The ancestral or proto-language reconstructed from these was called Indo-European. By the mid-nineteenth century the term Aryan was being used for those who spoke these languages. The name was derived from the Vedic *ārya* and the Avestan *airiia*.

These philological readings coincided with and were instrumental in European reconstructions of the past and present. By the late nineteenth century Social Darwinism – the adaptation of Darwinism to social history – was linked to what was emerging as 'race-science'. History was seen as involving the inter-action of races. This view became a further reason justifying high imperialism when the upper classes were said to be of the superior Aryan race. These theories touched some of the ideas that emerged from German Romanticism and culminated in Ariosophy and the Nazi ideology. This was also a view that undermined orthodox Christian theology. But by the middle of the twentieth century the fallacies of racial theories had become apparent and the theories were generally discarded by biologists and cultural historians. But they remained popular in India and continue to be.

IV

Early sources from India of the period under discussion do not use *ārya* in a racial sense. There is a consciousness of being an *ārya* and this is linked to upper-caste status in a system of *varṇa*-based society (*śudra*s are not *ārya*s); respectability of occupation or designation (scavengers are not *ārya*s); using the Sanskrit language where others use different languages; and worshipping the Vedic deities propitiated in hymns and initially as abstractions through sacrificial rituals, where others worship iconic or aniconic fertility and folk symbols through rituals other than large-scale sacrifices. Gradually as these characteristics broadened out and changed the connotation of *ārya* also changed. The Buddhist monk, essentially opposed to Vedic belief and ritual, breaking the rules of *varṇa*-based society, speaking Prakrit, is nevertheless addressed as '*ārya*' by lay Buddhists as a mark of respect.

The use of Aryan as a racial category in European and subsequently Indian discourse is incorrect. Aryan was initially the label of a language: the Indo-Aryan language. Therefore 'Aryan' technically refers to the 'the Indo-Aryan speaking people' and 'Aryan' is a short-cut for this label. Race and language cannot be confused since race is a biological category and language is a cultural and social category. Yet this confusion has persisted in the writings of many during the last hundred or more years and has become part of the definition of Aryan. The same criticism applies to the use of the term Dravidian race, where Dravidian is again a language label.

Max Müller interpreting Vedic texts, was a major exponent of the Aryan. Despite his recognizing the difference between race and language he often merged the two. He argued for a central Asian homeland of the Aryans and their branching into two, one moving towards Europe and the other to Iran. The latter split and one branch invaded northern India. He identified the Aryan and Aryan culture as the foundation of Indian civilization. This theory resounded across India in the late nineteenth century. It was a theory of empowerment, including some and excluding others. Hence the persistent concern to this day with identifying the Aryans.

The reconstruction of history varied in accordance with the ideological support sought from the theory. The range was enormous, as for example in the views of Jyotiba Phule, B. G. Tilak, Dayanand Saraswati or the Theosophical Society, all writing at about the same time in the late nineteenth century and some still being quoted as the mainspring of what are regarded today as 'indigenous' interpretations of Indian history. Needless to say that even the nineteenth century debate was not derived from indigenous theories and ideas. It was based on ideas developed in Europe and given exposure in India through colonial writings and these were then, in some cases, sieved through various nationalist ideologies. The irony is that the construction of the Aryan that emerged from these theories is now regarded entirely as an indigenous construction. That it drew from dialogues involving inputs from both the colonized and the colonial power is often forgotten.

Jyotiba Phule in Maharashtra argued that the Aryans invaded India and were the *brāhmaṇa*s who conquered the indigenous non-brahmanas and subjugated them by segregating them through imposing caste. His close contemporary B. G. Tilak had entirely different views and was closer to Max Müller's interpretations. Dayanand Saraswati was active in Gujarat and Punjab. He founded the Arya Samaj which called itself "The Society of the Aryan Race". Dayanand argued that the Aryans migrated from Tibet and were characterized by racial and linguistic purity. For him the finest religious articulation came from the *Veda*s to which the Hindus should return. And then there was the Theosophical Society founded in 1875 by the colourful Madame Blavatsky, and her associate Col. Olcott. It was closely aligned to the Arya Samaj for a brief period. Olcott was the first to maintain that the Aryans were indigenous to India, and this made it easier to argue as he did that they were ancestors to the modern Hindus.

These varied interpretations influenced public perceptions and were reflected in the ideas of Aurobindo, Vivekanada and others, none of whom were historians and therefore had a rather fluid view of evidence and chronology. These views were an attempt to reverse the colonial theory of the Aryans invading India and bringing civilization, rather as a proto-type of the later British colonial invasion. But Indian opinion did not address the more fundamental question, that of the construction of 'the Aryan' and its implications for the construction of an identity in India. Even today it is not the so-called school of indigenous interpreters that are addressing this question. They too assume the validity of the colonial and other nineteenth century constructions. Whatever questioning is being done is by scholars who critically enquire into constructions when analyzing evidence.

V

The picture was further complicated in the 1920s and 30s with the excavations of the cities of Harappa and Mohenjo-daro. Historians writing in the early half of the twentieth century agreed that the cities of the Indus plain preceded Vedic culture and that the two cultures were substantially different. It was also said that the Indus cities were attacked by the invading Aryans and hence their decline.

With extensive excavations after 1947 in both India and Pakistan, the archaeological picture has changed to some degree. The evolution of cultures – hunting, food-gathering, pastoralism, shifting agriculture, peasant economies and cities – is more easily traceable in various areas.

This process culminated in urban settlements in some areas which became the major Harappan cities in north-western India and Gujarat. The sites in Cholistan along the Hakra river which have been much discussed, do not give the impression of having preceded the Indus cities in gradually evolving towards urbanization but rather, that Mature Harappan settlements intruded into the area. It is because of the location of these sites that the Indus civilization is being referred to by a few archaeologists as the Sarasvati Civilisation, on the assumption that the Hakra river should be identified with the Sarasvati – an assumption that is by no means established. The most interesting aspect of these sites is that when urban decline began there was a migration towards Punjab and the Ganga-Yamuna doāb.

The identity of the Harappans remains uncertain and for many it hinges on the deciphering of their script. Unsuccessful attempts have been made to read it as a Dravidian or an Indo-Aryan language. There is now even a suggestion that it may not be a script but rather a representation of signs and symbols, since it has defied decipherment, a view that is still debated.

The extensive reach of the Indus civilization introduced contacts with central Asia, Afghanistan, the Indo-Iranian borderlands and settlements along the Persian Gulf. There is evidence of some coming and going of peoples of these regions, varying in intensity over the centuries. There is no evidence that an invasion of the cities by 'the Aryans' was the cause of their decline, but the possibility of encroachments and settlements of migrants, herders, incipient traders and such like, cannot be ruled out. Cities by their very nature are hubs of exchange and cannot sustain themselves if isolated.

The decline of the cities is now being attributed to various environmental changes. Among these are possible changes in the flow of the Indus near Mohenjo-daro which created permanent flood conditions, and the drying up of the Hakra river which once flowed parallel to the Satlej and the Indus with its estuary in the Rann of Kutch. These riverine changes seem to have occurred towards the early part of the second millennium BC. Conditions of deforestation and desiccation have also been suggested as well as changes in sea level. A decrease in trade would have led to de-urbanisation. It is important to remember that although the cities declined this did not necessarily mean the end of all aspects of the Harappan Culture. Some traits could well have continued in the cultures that were late contemporaries and then succeeded the earlier settlements such as the Painted Grey Ware Cultures in the Punjab and the Black-and-Red Ware cultures in Gujarat.

There was a fair amount of activity along the Indo-Iranian borderlands with some new cultures and cultural items coming down to the plains. These are visible by the end of the second and early first millennium BC in the Gandhara Grave Culture in the Swat valley, the Cemetery H Culture in the Punjab and the culture associated with Pirak in Baluchistan. There are numerable points within this geographical area through which exchanges of some degree took place. The post-Harappan cultures gradually introduced the use of iron and the horse became a familiar animal as did the chariot that accompanied it. The presence of the horse and the chariot if at all, in some Late Harappan sites was marginal. It was not characteristic of the culture as it came to be in post-Harappan Vedic sources.

VI

Among linguists the Vedic corpus was earlier used primarily for philological studies and later for what emerged as some aspects of linguistic studies, for the chronological and geographical location of words and texts and for possible bilingualism.

Philology involved syntax, morphology, phonetics, dialect changes and such like of the Indo-Aryan and linked languages. It was recognized that Indo-Aryan has a history of linguistic change and what has been called Old Indo-Aryan is different from Classical Sanskrit as discussed in Pāṇini. Vedic Sanskrit therefore requires a particular expertise.

The earliest form of Indo-Aryan which has been labeled as Proto-Indo-Aryan, is not to be found in India but in northern Syria and Anatolia. It is recorded in a treaty between the Hittites and the Mitannis which has been firmly dated to the fourteenth century BC. These fragments of Indo-Aryan survived for a brief while and then disappeared when the local languages asserted their dominance. Proto-Indo-Aryan cannot be said to have come from India as there is no connecting link between India and northern Syria. It has been suggested that both types of Indo-Aryan originated in the area between the Caspian and the Oxus and spread in different directions.

Another language which is a cognate of the Indo-Aryan of the *Ṛgveda* is the language of the *Avesta*, a Zoroastrian text of approximately the same period and the language of which is referred to sometimes as Old-Iranian. This again is closely related to Vedic Sanskrit but is now thought to be a little more archaic. The *Avesta* is currently being dated to about 1300 BC. The dual division of the *airiia* and the *dāha* in the *Avesta* is equated with the Vedic *ārya* and *dāsa*. The 's' and the 'h' are sometimes interchanged in the two languages.

Even within India the perspectives from linguistics are suggesting other ways of looking at the question different from the conventional. It has been argued that the Indo-Aryan of the *Ṛgveda* has elements of the Munda and Dravidian languages, suggesting not the subordination of non-Indo-Aryan speakers but more likely close inter-action with them. Some scholars have even suggested possible bilingualism. These linguistic elements are absent in the language of the *Avesta*, despite its being a cognate language. The source therefore is in India. Presumably the induction of non-Aryan linguistic elements in the language of the *Ṛgveda* occurred later than the composition of the *Avesta* if the latter is an earlier composition. The incorporation of non-Aryan elements into Indo-Aryan may have come through the interaction of Indo-Aryan speaking pastoralists with non-Indo-Aryan speaking farmers – from what has been called the symbiotic relationship between pastoralists and farmers: the animals feed off the stubble after the harvest and manure the fields. Interestingly there is a greater frequency of non-Aryan elements in the Vedic vocabulary relating to agriculture than to other activities.

A different kind of focus by linguists has been one on ascertaining the stratigraphy of the *Ṛgveda*: that is, which sections were composed first and which compositions were added later.

This 'literary archaeology' as it has been called is applied to early texts from all over the world. Adding bits to existing texts as interpolations is always tempting because by doing so recent ideas can be made to pass off as ancient and established ones. The *Mahābhārata* is also an example of this as was demonstrated by V. S. Sukthankar in the Critical Edition of the epic.

The hymns of the *Ṛgveda* were composed over a period of a few centuries before being compiled. The edition currently used was put together by Śākalya and dates to about 1000 BC or even a little later. There is now an approximate chronological order of the hymns and a historical treatment should observe this order. Sometimes commentaries are needed for more detailed explanations. One such is the commentary of Sāyaṇa written in the fourteenth century AD, a period rich in commentaries. It needs to be studied more fully than it has been because even if it is somewhat fanciful at times it does reflect the perspective of medieval thought on the *Ṛgveda*, a perspective different from our times.

What all these perspectives suggest is that it is difficult to date the early sections of the *Ṛgveda* to before about the fourteenth century BC. Therefore if the date of the *Ṛgveda* is to be taken back by 1500 years then there will be a serious conflict with the Proto-Indo-Aryan and Old-Iranian evidence and this conflict has no obvious solution. This is part of the reason why one argues that in order to analyze the identity and the chronology of 'the Aryan' in India there has to be a familiarity with the areas beyond India where Indo-Aryan and its cognates occur.

VII

The linguistic and cultural evidence suggests that the societies of north-eastern Iran and north-western India were close. It is now thought that the language from northern Syria and that from Iran is not later than that of the *Ṛgveda* and is believed to be slightly more archaic. It is possible that Aryan speakers came to north-western India in small groups as part of a pastoral circuit seeking fresh fields and pastures new. This activity of pastoralists across the Indo-Iranian borderlands into the plains was a continuous happening until recent times. Some may have settled and inter-acted with local groups hence the incorporation of some non-Indo-Aryan elements into Indo-Aryan. This was not an invasion so the process of historical change for all the societies that were in contact was different from what it would have been had it been an invasion. This difference requires that the historian now focus on fresh questions other than those based on nineteenth century concerns.

The earlier assumption was that there was a homogenous, uniform Aryan culture that spread over much of the northern sub-continent and later arrived in the peninsula. This view has now been questioned. Varying cultures existed and their forms as they evolved need investigation. This would involve a reconstruction of the diverse kinds of societies mentioned in the *Ṛgveda* and visible from archaeological data and their interaction, without necessarily labeling any single one as specifically Aryan. For example, some *brāhmaṇa*s are said to be *dāsyaḥ putra*, son of a *dāsa* woman, and therefore initially despised but later respected. Who were these and what does their emergence suggest? D. D. Kosambi thought some may have been descendents of Harappan priests and therefore were believed to have access to esoteric knowledge. If this suggestion is plausible, some myths and rites may have found their way into Vedic belief and practice. A striking social change is apparent in the way in which the *dāsa* is initially feared but later *dāsa* becomes the term for a slave. How did this change occur and which were the groups of people involved in this change?

Certain basic facts have to be kept in mind. Aryan cannot be identified as a race or a biological identity. The recent hunt for a solution through DNA tends to further complicate the issue and raise yet another set of questions. Can a linguistic cultural label be converted into a genetic identity? The language, Aryan, can be used by diverse ethnic groups. The speakers of the language are differentiated from those that cannot speak it or speak it incorrectly and for whom terms such as *mṛdhra-vāc* and *mleccha* are used. The archaeologist cannot identify the language of a culture if there is no writing or if the writing cannot be read. Therefore the archaeologist cannot identify an archaeological culture as 'Aryan'. We have to wait until the Harappa script is read before the proposed identification of the Harappans with the Aryans can be considered. At most the material objects from an excavation can be compared with what is described in a text. But this is at best an ambiguous procedure and does not provide firm evidence, since the readings of an excavation can vary. Archaeological evidence is not drawn on isolated artifacts that may resemble a description in a text but on a comparison of the systems that make up a culture.

For the historian the term *ārya* conveys status and therefore gradually comes to be accepted as an honorific. It signifies the language spoken, the social conventions observed as also some belief systems. Above all it is a status demanding respect. The popular definition of Aryan requires to be reformulated.

I have tried to indicate the kind of complexities involved in the history of this period, which will be further discussed in the essays that follow. The complexities arise not only from the diversity of sources that provide evidence of varying kinds, but also from the extensive and necessary layering of the arguments that go into the making of the reconstruction. 'Aryan' was defined in the nineteenth century and the definition still prevails. Now that the sources have become more extensive in terms of data, and the questions that can be asked of these sources have become more incisive and include new perspectives, inevitably the definition of Aryan will change. And, if this was not enough, there is the further need to cope with the ideological pulls that govern what is often propagated in aid of political mobilization rather than the comprehension of past societies.

My attempt in these essays is to trace the concept of the Aryan as it took form in the past two centuries and to suggest historically different ways of examining the evidence, rather than repeating what are now dated arguments. For those that see the investigation of this period of Indian history as an attempt at explaining and understanding the past, the investigation is of a historical process. As such it has to be subjected to the analyses and critical enquiries required of a historical process and not be treated as fertile ground for fantasies about the past.

Notes

1. E. E. Evans-Pritchard, *The Nuer*, Oxford 1940; *Nuer Religion*, Oxford 1956.
2. B. Lincoln, *Priests, Warriors and Cattle*, Los Angeles 1981.
3. D. D. Kosambi, *The Culture and Civilisation of Ancient India in its Historical Outline*, London 1965, pp. 40–52.
4. When speaking of a period of three millennia ago, the term India applies to the sub-continent and not to the boundaries of the present-day nation state.

A Bibliography of More Recent Publications

Allchin F. R., (ed.), *The Archaeology of Early Historic South Asia*, Cambridge 1995.

Anthony D., 'Current thoughts on the domestication of the horse in Asia', *South Asian Studies*, 1997, 315–18.

Anthony D. and D. Brown, 'The Origins of Horseback Riding', *Antiquity*, 991, 65, 22-38.

Bokonyi S., 'Horse remains from the Prehistoric site of Surkotada, Kutch, late 3rd millennium BC', *South Asian Studies* 1997, 13, 297–306.

Bronkhorst J. and M. M. Deshpande (eds.), *Aryan and non-Aryan in South Asia,* Cambridge 1999.

Bryant E., *The Quest for the Origins of Vedic Culture*, Delhi 2000.

Das R. P., 'The hunt for foreign words in the Ṛgveda', *Indo-Iranian Journal*, 1995, 38, pp. 207–238.

Erdosy G., (ed.), *The Indo-Aryans of Ancient South Asia: language, material culture and ethnicity,* New York 1995.

Hock H. H., 'Whose past is it? Linguistic Pre- and Early History and self-Identification in Modern South Asia', *Studies in the Linguistic Sciences*, 2000, 30, 2, 51-75.

— —, 'Pre-Ṛgvedic convergence between Indo-Aryan (Sanskrit) and Dravidian? A survey of the issues and controversies'. In J.E.M.Houben (ed.), *Ideology and Status of Sanskrit*, Leiden 1996.

Jarrige J-F. et M. Santoni, *Fouilles de Pirak*, Paris 1979.

— —, (ed.), *Les Cités oubliées de l'Indus*, Paris 1988.

Kenoyer J. M., *Indus Valley Civilization*, Karachi 1988.

Kosambi, D. D., *Introduction to the Study of Indian History*, Bombay 1956.

Kuiper F. B. J., *Aryans in the Ṛgveda*, Amsterdam 1991.

Lal B. B., (ed.), *The Earliest Civilization of South Asia*, Delhi 1997.

Lucas J. R. (ed.), *The People of South Asia: The Biological Anthropology of India, Pakistan and Nepal*, New York 1984.

Meadow R. H., (ed.), *Harappa Excavations 1986–90. A Multi-Disciplinary Approach to Third Millennium Urbanism*, Madison 1991.

Meadow R. H. and Ajita Patel, 'A comment on horse remains from Surkotada by Sandor Bokonyi', *South Asian Studies*, 1997, 13, 308-15.

Mughal M. R., *Ancient Cholistan, Archaeology and Architecture*, Lahore 1997.

Parpola A., 'The coming of the Aryans to Iran and India and the cultural and ethnic identity of the *dāsas*', *Studia Orientalia*, 1988, 64: 195–302.

— —, *Deciphering the Indus Script*, Cambridge 1994.

Possehl G., (ed.), *Harappan Civilization: A Recent Perspective*, New Delhi 1993 (rev. ed.).

Ratnagar S., *Enquiries into the Political Organisation of Harappan Society*, Pune 1991.

— —, *The End of the Great Harappan Tradition*, Delhi 2000.

Rawling, P., *Horses, Chariots and Indo-Europeans*, Budapest 2000.

Sharma, R. S., *Advent of the Aryans in India*, Delhi 2001.

Staal J. F., (ed.), *Agni. The Vedic Ritual of the Fire Altar*, Berkeley 1983.

Talageri S., *Aryan Invasion Theory and Indian Nationalism*, New Delhi 1993.

Thapar R. et al., *India: Historical Beginnings and the Concept of the Aryan*, New Delhi 2006.

Witzel, M. (ed.), *Inside the Texts Beyond the Texts*, Cambridge Mass. 1997.

Witzel M., 'Authochthonous Aryans? The evidence from Old Indian and Iranian texts', *Electronic Journal of Vedic Studies*, 2001, 7-3, pp. 1–93.

1.

The Historiography of the Concept of 'Aryan'

Early Views

If one seeks for a narrative of the beginnings of Indian history from Indian sources, such a narrative can be found in some of the *Purāṇas*. Written in the first millennium AD these *Purāṇas* claim to refer to events of some millennia earlier. The earth was ruled by Manus and during the time of the seventh there was a great flood when everything was submerged. Manu, advised by Viṣṇu, had built a boat to carry him and the seven sages through the flood. Viṣṇu took the form of a fish, and Manu tied the boat to its horn. The fish swam through the waters and lodged the boat safely on a mountain-top. When the water subsided Manu returned home. The progeny of Manu became the ancestors to many lineages. Later kings seeking aristocratic status traced themselves back to these. Subsequent to these lineages there is a sequential listing of historically known dynasties. The intention therefore is to reflect a degree of historical perception and not restrict the narrative to a recitation of mythology. The myth has its own interest in terms of parallels with similar stories from ancient west Asia (Thapar 1978) .

Significantly, this view of the beginnings of Indian history makes no mention of the original ancestors being 'Aryan', in part perhaps because the term 'Aryan' was not an ethnic label. The names in the descent lists of the *Purāṇa*s are not listed as Aryan or non-Aryan and the ancestry of some is distinctly uncertain. There was a traditional view therefore, in which 'the Aryan' is absent. This changes however, in the nineteenth century narrative of the past where 'the Aryan' emerges as foundational to Indian history and the central figure of the narrative. This later version draws on a different body of texts, namely the *Veda*s, the earliest of which preceded these *Purāṇa*s by about fifteen hundred years. The question then is that of what is being referred to by the term *ārya* in the *Veda*s, and subsequently in other texts, and how and why has the identity of 'the Aryan' been constructed and what changes has it undergone. This is not an academic question but central to how identities are constantly constructed and changed in every society throughout its history.

The *Veda*s were composed in a period earlier than that of the *Purāṇas*, and were therefore in modern times taken as the starting point of Indian history. The earliest *Veda* was the *Ṛgveda* and its hymns are dated to the latter part of the second millennium BC. Recently there has been an attempt to revive the theory that the date of the *Ṛgveda* can be taken back to the third millennium BC and it can be treated as the literary counterpart of the Indus culture. But this view has not found general acceptance. Apart from major problems of parallels and co-relations with archaeological evidence, this creates a long chronological hiatus between the first and the later three *Veda*s – the *Sāma, Yajur* and *Atharva* – as the dating of these to the first millennium BC remains firm. Further, parts of the later *Veda*s are an exegesis on some Ṛgvedic hymns such that they indicate closeness in time between the earliest and the later *Veda*s. There is also a geographic shift from the upper Indus plain and its western borderlands which is substantially the location of the *Ṛgveda,* to include the Gangetic plain in the later three *Vedas*. The latter reflect societies in which the contours of *varṇa* as status groups, of economic occupations, of elements of kingship and possibly even the rudimentary forms of state systems, are taking shape.

The Aryan identity was encouraged by the pre-eminence given to the *Vedas* by the brahmanical tradition which also ensured that they became the primary texts for European scholars working on Indian civilisation. But apart from this there was a more evident European context that gave form to the theory about the Aryans as it developed in the nineteenth century.

Officers of the East India Company serving in India began to explore the history and culture of the colony they were governing. This was both out of curiosity about governing a singularly alien culture and out of a conviction that an effective control over society required knowledge of its history, and if the knowledge was not readily available it would have to be discovered. The time was the late eighteenth century when the new ideas of the Enlightenment were in the air. Knowledge, when it was referred to as "the furniture of empire" was viewed as an access to power. Governing a colony required familiarity with the local languages, laws and religions since these were seen as the constituents of its culture. History was defined in accordance with Enlightenment definitions and such histories seemed not to be available in the corpus of Sanskrit literature, regarded as the pre-eminent intellectual corpus of the pre-colonial period. The history of early India therefore as now constructed would have an emphasis on tested chronology and sequential narrative.

Early explorations were dominated by the need to construct a chronology for the Indian past. Attempts were made to trace parallels with Biblical theories and chronology. But the exploration with the maximum potential lay in the study of languages and particularly Sanskrit. Interest in these studies was enhanced with the recognition that there were similarities between Sanskrit and the classical languages of Europe (Jones 1788). This had been referred to in previous centuries by merchants and missionaries visiting India. The most widely quoted among these was an Italian merchant Filippe Sassetti who in the sixteenth century suggested a link between Sanskrit and some European languages. These comments gave way to more systematic studies by Sir William Jones and his colleagues working in various administrative positions of the East India Company and who began researching into Sanskrit and the local languages such as Bengali, Urdu and Hindi in the late eighteenth and early nineteenth century.

William Jones was intrigued by what he saw as parallels between Greco-Roman deities and those of the Hindu pantheon as also by the possibility of comparing Biblical and Hindu mythological narratives to provide chronological clues. But his more lasting work was in the comparative study of languages. William Jones wrote not only on the excellent qualities of Sanskrit as a language but also argued that it was a cognate of Greek, Latin and Persian, and that all of them doubtless had a common ancestor. Sanskrit was not the parent language but it was one among six that probably were descended from an ancestral language. Terms such as 'Aryan' and Indo-European had not yet come into use. The notion of monogenesis – the single origin of all these languages – was extended to the speakers of the languages as well. This slippage between speech and biology was to dominate the nineteenth century.

At Chennai, somewhat later, the work of Ellis and still later Caldwell is associated with analytical studies of Telugu and Tamil (Ellis 1816, Caldwell 1856). The difference between what came to be known as the Indo-Aryan languages and the Dravidian languages was noted by both the British scholars and by those indigenous scholars – the pundits – who were providing information on Sanskrit and Telugu. What this pointed to was that Sanskrit was not ancestral to all the Indian languages and that the Dravidian group had other roots. Prior to the spread of Indo-Aryan, the Dravidian languages were used in various parts of the sub-continent as is also evident from linguistic remnants to this day. There was a borrowing between the various groups of languages which is as would be expected where they were being spoken in some proximity. The recognition that there were other languages contemporary with Indo-Aryan such as those of the Dravidian and Austro-Asiatic families required examining their relationships. In the early Tamil sources there are references to the *ariyar* as those who come from the north and this is taken as a reference to *ārya*s.

The possibility of comparing languages encouraged the evolution of philology in European universities and it became the forerunner to modern linguistics – the science of language. The Vedic corpus became available in the early nineteenth century to scholars in Europe and furthered the interest in comparative philology. These studies gradually envisaged an Indo-European family of languages descended from an ancestral language. The idea that the identity of speech and of people coincided meant that by the latter half of the nineteenth century European scholarship searched for the homeland of a people, the Indo-Europeans, a search in part encouraged by German Romanticism (Leslie Willson 1964, Drew 1987).

This was given a further impetus by the prevailing theory of discrete civilisations. The world was divided into self-sufficient civilisations demarcated by language and religion. India therefore was the civilisation of the Sanskrit language and the Hindu religion. Sanskrit was said to be the oldest surviving Indo-European language, although the proto-language had to be reconstructed through back formation from the later languages. However, this was an easy step to seeing Sanskrit as the ancestral language as some did and still do. German Romanticism was partial to this idea. Herder and Schlegel suggested that the roots of human history might go back to the beginnings recorded in Sanskrit texts.

Comparative philologists such as E. Burnouf and F. Bopp were primarily interested in the technicalities of analysing language. Philological studies delved into the grammatical structure of Pāṇini' s treatment of classical Sanskrit and this was in some ways new to European linguistic studies. Indo-European, reconstructed from the daughter languages, was traced back to a central Asian homeland. Europe was on the edge of an Oriental Renaissance. It was believed that yet another Renaissance might follow from the discovery of the Orient and this would take knowledge into yet other directions (Schwab 1984).

Those who spoke languages derived from Indo-European, came to be referred to by various labels, but ultimately 'Aryan' became the accepted one by the middle of the nineteenth century. The term was taken from references in the *Ṛgveda* where the authors of the hymns refer to themselves as *ārya,* and from the Iranian *Avesta* where the term *airiia* is used. In neither case was it used in a racial sense. *Ārya* in Sanskrit texts was used as an epithet of status particularly when the language itself became increasingly associated with status. For philologists Aryan indicated a language and therefore meant, 'an Aryan-speaking person'. This was frequently abbreviated to Aryan and came to be applied incorrectly as a racial label.

Association with Race

This interest in the Aryan coincided with the theories of the Comte de Gobineau who was searching for Aryan identities in Europe and warning against interbreeding between what were beginning to be described as Aryan and non-Aryan peoples (Poliakov 1974). Classification according to race was borrowed from biological studies such as the principles of Linnaeus for defining genera and species, as also the theory of the survival of the fittest, and both were applied to human societies. Races were arranged in a hierarchy of advanced and backward. What has been described as 'race-science' was viewed as an accurate identification of human groups (Stepan 1982). Race shifted the focus of Europe's origins from possible Biblical beginnings to what was thought of as the more 'scientific' understanding of origins in the form of races. In many ways race was invented by European colonialism. The demonstrated success of imperialism and the view that European nations were the most advanced, in contrast to the colonised who were thought of as the lesser breeds, reinforced these identities, as also did Social Darwinism. These ideas acted as a factor in changing the European view of its origins.

The intersection of Europe and Asia, and the resulting philological studies, initially in German and French thought, had earlier played with ideas of possible Oriental origins. German Romanticism in the earlier part of the nineteenth century portrayed Sanskrit and Indian culture as encapsulating the noble beginnings of universal civilisation. Sanskrit was described as the parent language and the Aryans of India as the fount of civilisation and from whom there was a dispersal of culture and language to other parts of the world. Asia became the focus of historical investigation.

Parallel to this another line of thinking developed in Germany. This was influenced by a search for origins and identities in the later nineteenth century. It had been argued that the Roman Empire declined from the fifth century AD because of frequent attacks by the German and other tribes on northern Europe who were regarded as barbarians by the Romans. These attributes of the tribes were gradually changed from their being barbaric to their being heroic and invincible, creating and defending the kingdoms they established in medieval times in northern Europe. A consciousness of pan-Germanism gradually took root. More importantly, Tacitus, a Roman historian of the first century AD who had written about the purity of blood of the German tribes was frequently quoted *(Germania,* 2; 4). Purity of blood became the criterion of racial superiority. The German tribes were said to constitute the original people, the *urvolk,* and their language was the original language, the *ursprache*. This demarcated them from other communities in Europe where both language and race had been contaminated.

Such ideas were common currency in much of Europe with various communities claiming the status of superior Aryans. The emerging nation-states were not always averse to the claims of Indo-European ancestry in race and language. The experience of colonial empires introduced a certain hesitation if not embarrassment at admitting to a common origin with some of the communities of Asia.

Given this, it was inevitable that the original Aryan would be geographically relocated and made a part of Europe. By the end of the nineteenth century the Aryans were divided into Asian and European. The former had their homeland in central Asia and the latter were said to have originated from the Nordic blondes of northern Europe (Taylor 1889). This was facilitated by the claim that the descendents of Indo-Europeans had diverse skull types as revealed by craniology. The measurement of the cephalic index and the nasal index as indicators of race was to be enthusiastically adopted in India, as for example in the activities and writings of Herbert Risley (Risley 1908).

The equation of language with race was made with increasing frequency. Its presence has also been noticed in the initial reconstruction of the history and civilisation of the ancient Greeks (Bernal 1987). Less credence was given to possible Mesopotamian and Egyptian antecedents with a preference for treating ancient Greek culture as an Aryan creation, introduced through the conquest of Greece by an Aryan people. From this point on the

Aryan became axiomatic to the study of human typology. It was to have disastrous consequences in twentieth century Germany with the Nazi ideology proclaiming the superiority of the Aryan race.

The theory of Aryan race was viewed as foundational to Indian history largely through what has been called the twinning of the theories of British Sanskritists and ethnographers (Trautmann 1997). Max Müller's influential role lay in his projecting Indian civilisation primarily through the prism of what he constructed as the culture of the *Vedas*. He edited the *Ṛgveda* and included the fourteenth century commentary on the text by Sāyaṇa. For Max Müller the *Ṛgveda* was the earliest stratum of Indo-European and therefore the most ancient literature in the world and the key to the earliest language and religion of India. He maintained that there was an original Aryan homeland in central Asia from where there was a dispersal of Aryan speakers branching off in two directions (Max Müller 1862, 1883, 1888). One went to Europe and the other migrated to Iran eventually splitting again with one segment invading north-western India. The references in the *Ṛgveda* to the *ārya*s and to their hostility towards the *dāsas* were read as the Aryans invading and enslaving the indigenes – the *dāsas*, and eventually settling in India. The reference to *ārya varṇa* and *dāsa varṇa*/*ārya* and *dāsa* colour, was understood to mean skin pigmentation and seen as a description of fair skinned Aryans conquering the dark-skinned aborigines. Despite his including the commentary of Sāyaṇa, Max Müller paid little attention to the explanations in the commentary. Admittedly these were fanciful at times but nevertheless they do indicate that there was no reference to race.

The northern Aryans who are said to have migrated to Europe are described by Max Müller as active and combative and ultimately gave expression to the idea of a nation. The southern Aryans who migrated to Iran and to India were passive and meditative, concerned with religion and philosophy. The two *varṇas* were said to be two conflicting groups differentiated by skin colour, language and religion, underlining racial differences. The *ārya*s developed Vedic Sanskrit as their language. The two were segregated through the instituting of caste. The upper caste Hindus were the biological, lineal descendents of the Aryans. The lower castes, untouchables and tribals were descended from the *dāsa*s. As was common in the nineteenth century Max Müller used a number of words interchangeably, such as Hindu/Indian, race/ nation/ people/ blood, words whose meanings would today be carefully differentiated.

Although in the ancient texts Aryan was specifically a label for a language and a social status, in the nineteenth century it came to be used indiscriminately for a race as well, both in Europe and in India. Max Müller denied any link between language and race, when he stated that, "Aryan in scientific language is utterly inapplicable to race. It means language and nothing but language ..." (Max Müller 1898; 90). But there was often confusion between language and race. It was thought that those who spoke the same language were inevitably members of the same biological race. History has proved this to be entirely erroneous. The same language can be spoken by members of more than one race or one ethnic group depending on the historical need for the language. Even Max Müller was given to confusing the two. Speaking on Ram Mohun Roy in 1883, he says, "Ram Mohun Roy was an Arya belonging to the south-eastern branch of the Aryan race and he spoke an Aryan language, the Bengali ... We recognise in Ram Mohun Roy's visit to England the meeting again of the two great branches of the Aryan race, after they had been separated so long that they had lost all recollection of their common origin, common language and common faith" (Max Müller 1984; 11). The sliding from language to race became frequent in contemporary thinking. An equally erroneous equation in South Asia was that of the Dravidian languages with a Dravidian race. The structure of Indo-

Aryan and Dravidian languages differed hence it was maintained that they represented a racial differentiation as well. Furthermore, it was held that since Indo-Aryan came from outside, the speakers of Dravidian were native to India.

The reconstruction of what was believed to be Aryan history superseded the initial eighteenth century Orientalist search for Biblical connections and parallels even in the early history of India. There was now briefly, a focus on common Aryan origins with Europe. This included a dismissal of the intervention of the Semitic peoples and languages, both in European and Indian culture. There was such an emphatic focus on the *Veda*s that even the *Purāṇa*s were for Max Müller second order knowledge. As we have seen the Puranic version of historical genesis did not involve *ārya*s and *dāsa*s or any ethnic overtones. The exclusion of the Semitic meant an exclusion of any Islamic contribution to Indian civilisation in the perspective of Max Müller. He refers to the tyranny of Mohammedan rule in India but does not explain why he thought it was tyrannical. This was a statement frequently made by British scholars. It is explained as implying that the Hindus were now rid of oppressive Muslim rule which had been replaced by benevolent British rule for which the Hindus would hopefully show appreciation (Elliot and Dowson, I, xxii).

The equation of language and race was instrumental in the formulating of the theory. Aryan conquest was seen as introducing both the Indo-Aryan language brought by people of the Aryan race and also what has come to be described as the distinctive Aryan civilisation. This became the opening narrative of Indian history. It was acceptable to historians who at the time often ascribed the explanation of events to conquest. The theory was attractive to colonial thinking because it provided an antecedent to the British conquest of India and the introduction of what was believed to be an imported civilisation through this process, a view which is partially responsible for the current rejection in some circles of the Aryans being other than indigenous.

It also assisted with another explanation. Racial separateness required a demarcating feature and conquest became the mechanism by which caste hierarchy and inequalities could be explained as a form of racial segregation. Since caste was central to Indian social institutions, racial segregation by this logic played the same role. Caste became more comprehensible if it was explained merely as racial segregation rather than by the more complex theories involving kinship, occupations, and rules of purity and pollution. Indian history was gradually being brought into the current European discourse on race.

The idea of the separation of the European from the Asian Aryans entered the discussion when colonial policy drew a sharp distinction between the coloniser and the colonised. The equality of European and Asian Aryans began slowly to be denied. Such a denial was necessary for those who proposed a radical social and economic restructuring of the colony through legislation and administration so that the colony would be converted into a viable source of revenue. Discussion on such matters was current among Utilitarian thinkers, the Free Trade lobby and economists such as Adam Smith. At the same time those who supported Orientalist views on the Indian past were sympathetic to the theory since it gave pre-eminence to the *brāhmaṇa*s and to their authorship of the *Veda*s. The *brāhmaṇa*s were thought to be the pre-eminent Aryans and this made the segregation of the Aryans from the non-Aryans more evident.

Since the identity and history of 'the Aryans' was said to be foundational to Indian history there was naturally considerable interest in the subject. European interest had been kindled both by the investigation of new knowledge through comparative philology as well as the politics of race-science in the age of imperialism, ideas that were thought of as relevant to European history as well.

The reaction in India was similar and the theory provoked a variety of ways of explaining the beginnings of Indian history. But much beyond that it provoked very diverse views about Indian society and the political outcome of these views was not only apparent at that time but often continues to this day. This had its parallels in Europe. Professional historians did attempt to maintain a distance from the broader implications but inevitably the shadow of the latter occasionally fell on scholarship as well.

Caste as racial segregation, separating the upper caste Aryan from the lower caste non-Aryan, was viewed as a scientific way of organising society in keeping with modern ideas. When the rigidity of caste was criticised, especially by missionaries, it was accepted that this weakened Indian society, particularly in its confrontation with Islam. Caste was divisive and therefore a united front against invaders was not possible – an argument that is still heard from people who forget that campaigns within India between Hindu rulers were equally destructive of the social fabric. It was also said that caste saved Hinduism from being absorbed into other religions and helped maintain its identity. There were few analyses where caste was seen to have its own history of adaptation and change. Moralising on the evils of caste precluded the need to see it as an agency of power, dominance and subordination, or to recognize the large area of negotiation which permitted some castes to shape their status.

The theory was popularised in India through the views of Max Müller. It was also taken up by those working on the early Sanskrit texts such as John Muir (1874) and John Wilson (1877). The latter, as missionaries, were critical of the inequities of caste and drew attention to the plight of the lower castes. They now argued that the lower castes who were the indigenous inhabitants were oppressed by the *brāhmaṇa*s who were the *ārya*s and came as invaders. There was a conflict between the *ārya* and the non-*ārya*.

The term *ārya* also came to be used as a patronymic referring to the Aryan people.

Some Indian Views of the Theory

Such views were becoming familiar to many Indians. Among them, a radical turn was provided by Jyotiba Phule whose perceptions were very different from the concerns of European comparative philologists and supporters of race-science. Writing in the latter half of the nineteenth century in Marathi, Phule argued that the original inhabitants of India were the *ādivāsī*s, among whom he included the *śudras, ati-śudras* and Dalits, all of whom were descendents of the heroic peoples led by the *daitya* king, Bali (G. P. Deshpande 2002). Various such categories were included under the generic title of *kṣatriya*. The *ādivāsī*s fought the arrival of the *brāhmaṇa*s who represented the Aryans, but were conquered and subordinated. Phule draws on well-known myths to emphasise his point. (His views are discussed further in Essay 2).

Phule's version has become essential to the Dalit perspective on Indian history. It was also to influence a number of the non-Brahmin Movements in the peninsula. The dichotomy between Brahmin and non-Brahmin slid easily into the linguistic division of Aryan and Dravidian languages where the former language was of the former group and the latter language of the latter groups. The language demarcation was an important component of the social divide (Ramaswamy 1997). The rejection of Aryan dominance implied a rejection of the Indo-Aryan languages. Phule's interpretation of the theory made caste the differentiating feature rather than race or religion in explaining the beginnings of history. In this interpretation the lower castes had a chronological priority in their identity with the land.

The upper castes had their own use for the theory of Aryan race and it was again given a turn that suited their social aspirations and political needs. The views of Phule were generally ignored. B.

G.Tilak, also from Maharashtra but writing in English, endorsed the antiquity of the *Ṛgveda* by taking it back to 4500 BC, considerably earlier than the date of 1500 BC given by Max Müller. Tilak based his argument on his readings of what he claimed were planetary positions referred to in the hymns (Tilak 1893, 1903). Accepting the theory of the Nordic homeland for European Aryans, Tilak maintained that the Aryans had trekked from the Arctic in the post-glacial age and then branched off, one group settling in Europe and the other travelling to the Indian sub-continent. The European Aryans relapsed into barbarism, but those that settled in India retained their original superior culture which they imposed on the local non-Aryans. The introduction of geology into the argument created other complications. Some time later when objections were raised to Tilak having supported the theory that the Aryans came from outside India, the objections were set aside by some people arguing that in those early times the North Pole was within the territory of British India! (Das 1920). Max Müller was familiar with Tilak's ideas although not in agreement with them, but he did incidentally help in getting Tilak released from jail when he was incarcerated for nationalist activities.

The theory was used by some to argue for the superiority of the upper castes and to promote their self-esteem by maintaining that not only were the upper castes the lineal descendants of the Aryans but that they were also racially related to the European Aryan. Keshab Chunder Sen follows Max Müller and John Wilson when he states that, " ... in the advent of the English nation in India we see a reunion of parted cousins, the descendants of two different families of the ancient Aryan race" (Sen, 323). The theory of common origins strengthened a possible link between the colonisers and the Indian elite. The superiority of the Aryan was an inheritance from nineteenth century theories and is one of the factors in the current insistence that the Aryan should be indigenous to India.

Views such as these coincided with the emergence of nationalism in the late nineteenth century articulated mainly by the middle class, drawn from the upper castes. In a period of rapid social change even these groups were seeking both legitimacy and identity from the past. Origins therefore became crucial. Aryan origins and lineal descent was emphasised and appropriated by the upper castes. Other castes and non-Hindus were either marginalised or excluded. Aryanism therefore became an exclusive status conditioned by birth. Biological status was coming back through a circuitous way and the qualification of language was receding. Nevertheless Aryan and non-Aryan differentiation which had been of an ethnic and racial kind was also beginning to touch implicitly on class differentiation.

Nationalisms of various kinds – anti-colonial, religious, regional, linguistic – demand theories of origins and identities, perhaps more insistently than other political movements. These theories resort to their versions of history and particularly the beginnings of history, drawing attention to when a society believes it was founded. Therefore, Aryanism having become foundational to Indian history, new nationalisms reinterpreted the theories to support their political aspirations.

The reverse but parallel image as it were of Phule' s thesis was that expounded by Dayanand Saraswati, a *brāhmaṇa* learned in the *śastra*s and who has also been described as a social reformer. He founded the Arya Samaj, an organisation seeking to return to what it interpreted as the social and religious life of the *Veda*s. These texts became the blue-print of Dayanand's vision of Indian society as set out in his best known work, *Satyartha Prakash*. He argued that the *Veda*s are the source of all knowledge including modern science. He underlined the linguistic and racial purity of the Aryans. The Arya Samaj was described by its followers as "the society of the Aryan race". The upper castes were the Aryas. Dalits were excluded, but through the innovation of a ritual called *shuddhi* or purification, it was possible for some lower castes to improve their caste status. The notion of their having to go through 'purification' is an indication of upper caste contempt. Dayanand stated that the Aryans, the authors of the *Veda*s, migrated into India from Tibet, although there was no evidence to suggest this connection with Tibet.

Dayanand had parleyed with another group that had firm ideas about the Aryans and the beginnings of Indian history. For a brief while the Theosophical Society and the Arya Samaj were virtually merged, but soon they fell apart. Neither Madame Blavatsky and Col. Olcott who founded the Theosophical Society in 1875, nor Dayanand, were exactly people who easily accommodated themselves to divergent views. Madame Blavatsky spent much of her time establishing centres in different parts of the world in order to legitimise her version of the occult. She fostered, however briefly, an interest in current nationalisms such as in Ireland and India. But her more lasting imprint was on centres in Europe that nurtured Ariosophist thinking involved with notions of Aryan superiority. Such centres were often the crucible of Aryan racism (Goodrick-Clarke 1992). In India the more active person was Col. Olcott. He regarded the Aryans as the ancestors of modern Hindus, and as indigenous to India, and that these same Aryans had been the progenitors of European civilisation (Leopold 1970, 1974). This was an echo of some of the earlier ideas of German Romanticism in relation to India. Theosophical views of this variety emerged out of what was believed to be an aura of oriental religions as well as the supposed dichotomy between the spiritualism of India and the materialism of Europe.

These varied versions of the theory and the issues that they were concerned with did not die out at the end of the nineteenth century but have lived vicariously through some of the social movements and political ideologies of the twentieth century. For example, the current notion being propagated that Hindus are descended from indigenous Aryans, was earlier expressed in the Theosophical reading of the Aryan theory as argued by Col. Olcott. The theory that the Aryans took civilisation from India to the west is being repeated. It is also said that Indian communities lived in harmony with each other and contentions came only with the arrival of 'the Muslims'.

Some authors writing at the popular level in the early twentieth century, redefined the Indian and the Aryan identity to give priority to a religious identity. Caste Hindus were Aryans and Aryans were indigenous to India. Non-Hindus were foreign and these were the Muslims, Christians, Parsis – and the Communists as well. All these were aliens since India was neither the land of their birth and ancestry – *pitṛbhūmi* – nor the place where their religion originated – *puṇyabhūmi* (Savarkar 1922, Golwalkar 1938). There had been at one point a collapsing of the racial identity with nationalism and at another a shift from race to caste. The use of the word *jāti* for both caste and race added to the confusion. Although *jāti* is linked to birth it also draws on a variety of social and religious activities which continually change the parameters of *jāti* identity. The racial identity is so deeply ingrained in the concept of the Aryan that references to 'the Aryan race' are common in the media and in the conversation of large numbers of people in India. However when the identity shifted to a more clearly religious one as in the equation of Aryan with Hindu, as it has now done, then the meaning of Aryan also changed, although the fuzziness often continues.

This range of interpretations of the Aryan theory illustrates how it came to be used in the agendas of various social groups and their contestations. It reflects an imagined ethnicity being presented as an explanation for the organisation of a society. The explanation takes on the colouration of scientific approval where biological heredity is made to coincide with categories of language. The history of a nation is sought to be traced with authority vesting in contemporary upper castes or those of the dominant religion. Alternatively a demand is made for the restitution of rights of those who see themselves as having been denied their claim to being the true inheritors of the land. Identities of race, caste and religion underline separateness. They also attempt to provide seemingly easy explanations of social insecurities, however invalid these may be as historical explanations.

The Entry of the Indus Civilisation

These varied versions of the theory faced another set of problems with the archaeological discovery of the Indus civilisation and its cities from 1922-23 onwards. The excavation of the cities of Harappa and Mohenjo-daro and subsequent excavations in India and Pakistan revealing an extensive urban culture distributed across the Indus plain and into Gujarat, created problems for the earlier simpler versions of the Aryan theory. The cities were found to date to the early third millennium and were therefore the culture that initiated Indian civilisation. Being predominantly urban the Indus civilisation is viewed by most scholars as distinctively different from the agro-pastoralists familiar from the *Veda*s and particularly the *Ṛgveda*. The *Veda*s are primarily ritual texts so their representation of society is somewhat indirect. The archaeological evidence, and particularly data relating to environment, technology and economy, covers a wider area and goes further back in time, and because it is most commonly in the form of an artefact it has precision. It has therefore come to be seen as the primary data for the reconstruction of the earliest history of India. This creates a problem for those who would still like to see the Vedic corpus as the earliest evidence of Indian history. Because these texts were used in reconstructing history prior to the discovery of the archaeological evidence, there is a tendency for the archaeological data to be read in the light of the Vedic corpus.

The idea of identifying the Indus cities with the authors of Vedic culture was again initially put forward by L. A. Wadell in 1925, working on Sumerian links but bringing in current readings of the role of the Aryan (Wadell 1925). Other archaeologists thought that the cities may have been built by pre-Aryans and subsequently destroyed by the Aryans. The discovery of the Indus cities was also used, to the contrary, as grist to the mill of Dravidian nationalism claiming that the Harappans were Dravidian speaking and that the civilisational roots of India were therefore Dravidian (Ramaswamy). This remains an undercurrent in the identification of the Indus civilisation. The claim tends to be rather brushed aside by the much more vocal insistence on Indo-Aryan roots through identifying the authors of the Harappan Culture with the Aryans who composed the *Ṛgveda*.

In pursuing the various ways in which the Aryan theory was used it is often forgotten that professional Indian historians tended to distance themselves from popular theories. Discussions of Indian views of the Aryans seldom quote historians but frequently quote Aurobindo, Vivekananda, Dayanand and Tilak, who were primarily philosophers and scientists, with political interests. They are sometimes described as representing the age-old Hindu intellectual tradition, a statement that overlooks the fact that they were essentially arguing within a colonial dialogue. The focus on roots and traditions did not draw on Sāyaṇa and his predecessors but was in the context of various contemporary nationalisms. The mix of anti-colonialism and religious revivalism varied in these nationalisms. Historians were not claiming to represent a tradition. The classic history by Hemchandra Raychaudhuri first published in 1923, *Political History of Ancient India*, begins with the accession of Parīkṣit, subsequent to the war in the *Mahābhārata*, and there is an association with the supposed start of the Kaliyuga after the war. Almost throughout the twentieth century historians kept a close tack on the evidence being revealed by excavations and the reading of the texts: the two technical interests that allowed them to explore historical beginnings. However, what was left unaddressed was the more fundamental question of the colonial construction of the Aryan identity and the implications of this construction for Indian history.

After the discovery of the Indus cities most histories began by describing them as the starting point of Indian civilisation and then proceeded to speak of a Vedic age as the successor. The rise of the cities were dated to the third millennium BC and the *Ṛgveda* to anywhere between 1500 and 1200 BC. The cultural identity of the Indus cities remained uncertain, but the coming of 'the Aryans' was attributed to an invasion. Max Müller's theory of an invasion was re-iterated by Mortimer Wheeler in his work on the archaeology of the cities. But gradually, the inter-weaving of archaeological and linguistic data – to the extent that this was possible – began to question such an invasion. With historical analysis increasingly approximating the methods of the social sciences, invasion as the invariable cause of historical change was being eroded. The linguistic evidence in particular pointed towards multiple small migrations and other changes in the cultural landscape of those times (Thapar, 1969, 1989-91).

In Europe scholars began to move away from pursuing origins and identities and broadened the parameters of Indo-European studies to include many more societies using languages associated with Indo-European. Although the study of comparative philology continued there was an added interest in comparative mythology. The exclusiveness of a single language group began to be questioned by the suggestion that there was a recognisable structural similarity and shared ideology across a spectrum of societies using languages of the Indo-European family. This, according to Georges Dumezil was expressed in a common pattern of social organisation which he called the Three Orders – priests, a warrior aristocracy and the pastoralists and cultivators – which was present in the mythology of these groups. Myths reflected the function of each group (Scott Littleton 1973). Although it was demonstrated that the theory of the Three Orders could be applied to non-Indo-European using societies as well, and therefore did not have a specificity relating to particular language groups, it did nevertheless, shift the sights of research to new perspectives. The archaeological hunt for the Aryans became less insistent. But the search for the Indo-European homeland continued. Maria Gimbutas suggested that the kurgan graves of central Asia were associated with the Indo-European speakers (Gimbutas 1997). Colin Renfrew argued for the diffusion of farming communities from Anatolia in preference to horse-riding and chariot using elites spreading from central Asia (Renfrew 1987). Neither of these hypotheses has however, provided the answer.

In India the attempt to co-relate archaeological and textual data took other forms. From the middle of the century when information from excavations was increasing, it began to be juxtaposed to the textual information of the earliest texts. Initially there was a bifurcation between histories based on the two categories of sources but attempts began to be made to integrate the evidence, which of course was difficult in most cases. The reading of archaeological evidence, as indeed of linguistic evidence as well, has its own rules. This is something that is not always remembered. Furthermore if the evidence from archaeology differs from that which comes from textual sources the attempt should not be to force a fit between the two but rather to try and understand what the evidence from each may be saying. This also requires that in commenting on these sources we need to be familiar with recent discoveries and interpretations and the rigour of the discipline in question.

The need therefore is to understand the parameters of the Harappan cities and not just to relate stray items of material culture to objects described in textual sources. There are a number of problems that have to be contended with in suggesting a co-relation. The geographical boundaries of the city civilisation extend far beyond those of the *Ṛgveda,* going south to Gujarat. The Indus cities as urban centres were dependent on a substantial agrarian production and agro-pastoral production alone would not have sufficed. This is attested by plough agriculture and granaries. A gradual change from village settlement to urban centre can be observed in association with the cities, as for example, in Baluchistan. Monumental structures are built on extensive brick platforms; the city-plan is carefully worked out including a remarkable system of drainage; there are impressive fortifications and the residential area has large familial houses with civic amenities. They were centres of craft production, linked to local and long distance trade. All this required arrangements for obtaining and controlling labour, gathering raw material, organising production and networks of exchange. The symbols on the seals and elsewhere have been taken as indications of a script, used presumably for identifying persons and products.

Such parameters are not recognisable in the *Ṛgveda*. This text is a collection of hymns yet even the religious articulation of these find little co-relation with artefacts from the cities (Thapar 1983). However significant and evocative the hymns of the *Ṛgveda* may be, and many are associated with early stages of religious belief and ritual, the societies that can be visualised through them are of relatively small groups of agro-pastoralists, living in villages, herding cattle and tending fields. Their wealth is computed in horses and cows hence the importance of the cattle-raid as an activity and the frequency of skirmishes probably over pastures and water sources. The horse had enormous functional importance as well as a ritual presence. Movements of people can occasionally be inferred and generally were from the north-west towards the Indo-Gangetic watershed (Thapar 2000).

The discussion on the chronological priority and the identity of the Indus civilisation and the Vedic corpus entered standard histories from the middle of the last century. The first volume of the History and Culture of the Indian People, entitled *The Vedic Age*, has references to this discussion (R. C. Majumdar, et al. 1951). It was initially a matter of historical interpretation often linked to the juxtaposition of data. But by the last decade of the century some of the discussion began to incorporate political intentions. If now it is to avoid becoming self-defeating, it is necessary that it remain a scholarly debate and that the parameters of historical methodology be observed.

Historical questions regarding Aryan identities are now enmeshed in a variety of cultural politics. The theory of the indigenous origin of Aryans in India was claimed by a particular ideology asserting a Hindu nationalism and seeking to negate much of the earlier scholarly arguments. Some of the arguments to support these theories tend to set aside scholarly analysis and focus on the claims being made. But there also is now among some other scholars an attitude bordering on condescension towards these views by arguing that in a post-colonial context theories emerging from such 'nationalisms' must receive serious attention not necessarily as scholarship but as nationalism. Further, that excluding them from discussion is contributing to a sort of Indological McCarthyism where the challenging of long-held assumptions pertaining to the Indo-Aryans are dubbed fundamentalist, nationalist and contributing to Nazi agendas (Bryant 2001; 276). Are we then to concede to the academic fashions that maintain that all theories of explanation have equal validity and should receive equal attention; or that earlier theories having arisen in a colonial context, contemporary theories coming from 'nationalist' concerns have to be given the benefit of doubt – even if such theories are borrowing from colonial interpretations that now have little scholarly validity? Such concessions are not conducive to advancing knowledge as has been argued persuasively by more than one commentator (Nanda 2003). Nor can the discussion of Vedic origins be reduced to a debate between 'westerners' and 'Indians' as some would have it. This does the debate an injustice. The theory has been used for all manner of purposes by 'westerners' and 'Indians' in the past. At least in present times it is possible to demarcate the scholarly from the non-scholarly pursuit, irrespective of whether the person is a 'westerner' or an 'Indian'. This should be the basis of the debate.

The two main issues on which the debate has focussed are chronology and identity. But as these essays will indicate much else has come under investigation and has resulted in historically stimulating questions. The chronological question has been whittled down largely to the date of the *Ṛgveda*. The generally accepted view is that it cannot be dated earlier than about 1500 BC on linguistic grounds especially now that comparative studies with contemporary Indo-Aryan and Indo-Iranian texts have been made more precise. The Indo-Aryan words in the Mitanni-Hittite treaty of the fourteenth century BC in Anatolia (also referred to as Proto-Indo-Aryan), and the Gāthā sections of the *Avesta*, both have some linguistic forms that are thought to be more archaic than the *Ṛgveda*. The date given in the treaty of the fourteenth century BC, is a useful chronological peg.

The earliest form of Indo-Aryan which has been labelled Proto-Indo-Aryan comes from West Asia and occurs in a treaty between the Hittites and the Mitannis at the termination of their conflict. The Hittites call upon their gods to witness the treaty and name them as Mitrashil, Uruvanshil, Indurah, Nashatyana. These occur in the *Ṛgveda* as Mitra, Varuna, Indra and Nasatya. The names are not identical with Vedic Indo-Aryan but are close and are thought to be an older form. This would date the *Ṛgveda* to slightly later than the fourteenth century BC. There are also some other words linked to the training of horses. The presence of horses was new to west Asia since they arrived there from central Asia, at the start of the second millennium BC, as they did elsewhere in the region. These fragments of Indo-Aryan survived for a brief while and then disappeared when the local languages asserted their dominance. Proto-Indo-Aryan cannot be said to have come from India as there is no connecting link, neither archaeological nor linguistic, between India and northern Syria. It has been suggested that both types of Indo-Aryan originated in the area between the Caspian Sea and the Oxus and spread in diverse directions (Burrow 1973).

Another language which is a cognate of the language of the *Ṛgveda* is Old Iranian, the language of the *Avesta,* a Zoroastrian text of approximately the same period. The *Avesta* is currently being dated to about 1300 BC and its language is now thought to be somewhat more archaic than that of the *Ṛgveda*. Apart from language there are also other similarities. Mithra and Varuna are important deities in the *Avesta* as they were in the *Ṛgveda* prior to the ascendence of Indra and Agni. But Indra is not a sympathetic deity in the *Avesta*. Some names and concepts are virtually the same in the two languages although curiously their meanings are reversed. Thus the Avestan *daeva* has the opposite connotation to the Ṛgvedic *deva*. Similarly the Avestan *ahura* is the great beneficial spirit although the word is the linguistic counterpart to the Ṛgvedic *asura*. The dual division of the *airiia* and the *daha* is the equivalent of the Vedic *ārya* and *dāsa*. The 's' and the 'h' are interchangeable in the two languages. The cult of *soma,* the hallucinogen that is ritually consumed in the course of some Vedic sacrifices is also important to the *Avesta* and known as *hoama*. Interestingly it does not occur as a ritual in the rites associated with other Indo-Europēan speakers.

There are other similarities that suggest a closeness of cultures. Both were agro-pastoral societies and primarily cattle-keepers. They show little familiarity with urban centres and the economies of production and exchange associated with such centres. There are no descriptions of monumental structures or the areas of a city such as are associated with urban settlements. Wealth is computed in animals particularly horses and cows. Horses were relatively new to this area which might explain why they are not depicted on the Harappan seals whereas the bull is common. The eating of cattle flesh was restricted to ritual occasions and this is an important characteristic of pastoral societies. Migrations are explicitly mentioned in the *Avesta* as well as the direction of the migrations. The reconstruction of the Iranian society of this period would have a bearing on the reconstruction of society across the borderlands in northern India.

By this time, c. 1300 BC, the Indus cities which preceded the *Ṛgveda* had declined. If there is an insistence that Indian civilisation has to have Aryan foundations then obviously the *Ṛgveda* as the earliest evidence of an Aryan presence has to be either prior to or contemporary with the Indus cities. Hence the suggestion that the *Ṛgveda* be dated a couple of thousand years earlier than the date accepted so far and that the language and culture of the Indus cities be taken as Aryan. But the evidence for this is not forthcoming.

Astronomy has been introduced into the discussion on the chronology of the *Ṛgveda*. H. Jacobi argued a century ago for an early date on the basis of what he read as references to planetary positions (Jacobi 1895). Modern aids to assess possible astronomical data have been suggested but without arriving at a conclusive date (Narahari Achar 1999). Recent views have questioned the claim that the Vedic Corpus which has references to the *saptarṣi*/Ursa Major in the far north and the *Kṛttikas*/Pleiades in the east, were composed in c. 3000 BCE (Witzel 1999, Parpola 1994). Furthermore, information from much earlier times can get embedded in ritual and through this channel continue into later times, as we know from texts of the historical period. But this does not date the text to an early period. Evidence from astronomy therefore is problematic. The nature of the Ṛgvedic hymns is such that it is difficult to put them in a chronological order. They are essentially ritual compositions and in some passages deliberately anachronistic as I have attempted to show with reference to techniques of making pottery (in Essay 5).

Although the re-examination of the evidence from archaeology has resulted in the discarding of the earlier notion of a systematic destruction of Harappan cities by Aryan invaders, this does not automatically lead to the corollary that the speakers of Indo-Aryan were indigenous to India. Indo-Aryan became the dominant language but the historical process by which this happened still needs to be explored. It was not an isolated language that evolved within the confines of the upper Indus plain. It had close cognates in Iran where it was also dominant and remained so, and in Anatolia where it faded out. The cultural history of these three regions has a bearing on the presence of Aryan languages in the wider area. The links with Old Iranian and the language of the *Avesta* suggest more than just a linguistic affinity with Indo-Aryan. It has long been pointed out that parallels from Iran occur in rituals, deities and social forms but the reversal of meaning in some cases suggests a statement of cultural demarcation by the two. The interaction of peoples, even small groups through their languages and cultures, over a period of time that extends into centuries, brings its own mutations. The demarcation possibly led to the language and concepts of Old Iranian and Indo-Aryan mutating independently in different habitats. Small migrations over long durations are not as visible as are massive movements but all the same they can be effective mechanisms of change.

Languages travel and are picked up or discarded for a variety of reasons arising from complex relationships. Exchanges of various kinds and the movements of peoples that this implies, however small in number, are means of transactions that are not always obvious. Pastoral circuits for example, can involve large herds of animals, fewer humans but a regularity of contact that could well bring about exchange and bilingualism. Historians have to consider typologies of exchange, migration, technology, and relationships that occur particularly in areas between well-defined regions, such as those on either side of the Indo-Iranian borderlands. Archaeological data can sometimes provide clues to these if stray artefacts suggest exchange or movement. Even if it is argued that Indo-Aryan was indigenous to India, (although the viability of the argument still remains to be established), the evolution of the language in terms of why it incorporated other linguistic forms from other indigenous languages needs to be explained. The fact that the Harappan trader, irrespective of what his own language might have been, had to speak a variety of other languages in the many areas where he traded, would have had some affect on his own language.

Single items in themselves do not necessarily tell us much such as the earliest horse bones in north-western India dating to the second millennium BC. A handful of horse bones scattered at various sites do not add up to a culture centred on the horse. The difference even in the numbers of bones between those found in Late Harappan levels and those found at other sites of the first millennium BC indicates which cultures were centred on the horse.

Further Aspects for Investigation

There are many summaries of existing opinions – short and long – and these keep getting repeated without too much attempt at considering new perspectives. This might suggest that leads of different kinds should be followed up instead of just the ones we are familiar with. The debate on origins and identities can be investigated through other aspects of the history of this period.

Potentially important recent archaeological discoveries have been the excavations of the Bactro-Margiana Archaeological Complex – BMAC – or what has been called the Oxus Civilisation, stretching from the Caspian to the Pamirs and active in the period from 2300-1900 but less active in the subsequent period until 1500 BCE. (Sarianidi 1999, Francfort 2005, Hiebert 1994). The BMAC had links with the Iranian plateau, Baluchistan and the Indus borderlands, and the Steppes of central Asia. It was one of the early crossroads of Asia. It was partly contemporary with the period of the Harappan cities and had its own urban centres in its oases. Some items produced here as prestige goods travelled to Baluchistan, Iran and the borderlands nearby. Anatolia would also have been accessible. Were these items of trade or were they items of gift exchange, since either would make a difference to the nature of the relationships involved in the exchange? Connections are also attested by the location of a Harappan settlement at Shortughai. The period of decline of the BMAC coincides interestingly with the decline of Harappan urbanism and changes in the wider area which had earlier been linked. Despite its proximity to cultures thought to have been Indo-European speaking, it remains unclear whether the BMAC used an Indo-European language since written records have not been found.

The decline in exchange between the urban centres may have encouraged a more marked presence of agro-pastoralists – a pattern not unfamiliar to later history (Fussman 2005). Their presence is evident from textual sources dating to the period when the BMAC was not so active. The Gāthā sections of the *Avesta* are now said to be earlier than had been assumed (Kellens 2005) with a date of the mid-second millennium BC or soon thereafter. The language is thought to be more archaic than that of the *Ṛgveda*. There are some echoes of the movement of peoples and perhaps languages in later Avestan with references to the lands created by Ahura Mazda and associated with the *airiia*. These are listed from the northernmost, Airiianem Vaego, coming south to Helmand and still further to Hapta Hindhu/Sapta Sindhu and its vicinity (Darmesteter, *Vendidad*, Fargard 1.4).

Pastoral groups may have been part of a central Asian cultural nexus which in the course of segmenting and moving also manifested local differences. The widening of pastoral circuits and the resulting interface with new societies and cultures would have affected the forms and structures of the earlier society. Ecological similarities would have encouraged diffusion but unfamiliar environments would have created some diversity. What were the factors that encouraged the widening of the pastoral circuits, if that is what happened? Was it a search for pastures and fresh water sources in a possible period of drought? Was it a demographic alteration? The relations between the societies of the *Avesta* and the *Ṛgveda* can be meaningfully explored to search for answers to such questions as can the archaeology of the regions familiar to these societies.

It is perhaps worth reminding ourselves that there were no political borders in those days and movements across geographical borderlands were not controlled by political boundaries. The boundary of the territories of British India cannot be the criterion for what is indigenous and what is alien to India. The presence of material objects in the archaeological record and their chronologies and distribution define cultures, as does the linguistic structure of the languages of the texts and the geographical direction taken by language and textual sources. Non-Indo-Aryan linguistic forms in the *Ṛgveda* (M. M. Deshpande 1979, Kuiper 1991) register contact between speakers of various languages. The types of linguistic importations could point to activities associated with specific languages and their speakers. It was suggested that tools used in agriculture tend to come from non-Indo-Aryan languages, such as Dravidian or/and Austro-Asiatic (Burrow 1973, 373 ff; Kuiper 1991). A fuller investigation of this might provide some worthwhile explanations of the social interface.

There needs to be a sharper definition of concepts such as chiefships and kingships as applied to the history of these times.

The activities of the *rājā* in the *Ṛgveda,* for instance, agree more closely with those of a chief of the clan rather than a king. The institutions associated with chiefships such as *samiti*s and *vidatha*s are not characteristic institutions of kingship; and *sabhā*s are different kinds of bodies in the two systems (Thapar 1984, 2000). The differentiation can also be sought in the sites where material could indicate differences. Urbanism is a distinctive change from previous settlements. Proof of urbanism requires evidence of many aspects of its functions – economic, administrative, and social to say the least – as is apparent from the excavations of the Harappan cities. It does not lie only in maintaining (incorrectly) that the word *pur* as it occurs in the *Ṛgveda* has the same meaning as the *pura* in later texts.

Sharpening definitions of forms of authority would require other data such as the juxtaposition of pastoralism and agriculture and the nature of reciprocal exchange. Did the juxtaposition for instance, in places where the pastoralists and the farmers had a symbiotic relationship as seen in animal herds grazing on the harvest stubble, bring about the borrowing of linguistic features from one language to another? Chiefdoms rely more on exchange of various kinds being reciprocal where items exchanged need not be identical but their evaluation is seen as equivalent. Kingdoms tend to rely more on nurturing dominant groups which help in controlling subordinate groups. The hierarchy of power is more complex. The seemingly egalitarian distribution of booty among clansmen after a raid, with some concession to a more substantial share for the priest and the *rājā*, would be gradually replaced by the inequities of the induction of labour to ensure an income for the chief. This would change the nature of relationships. A statement such as, the *kṣatr*/personifying power, eats the *viś*/the clansmen, in the same way as the deer eats grain, is obviously saying something about the system of control and not merely making a comparison (*Śatapatha Brāhmaṇa,* 8.7.1.2., 8.7.2.2., 9.4.3.5.). Monitoring changes such as these could be co-related with change in language or material culture.

The historical reconstruction of this period now presents a different picture from earlier theories. The identification of archaeological cultures as 'Aryan' without the evidence of writing was methodologically doubtful and has now become more so. There is no necessary co-relation between language and archaeological artefacts, although there can be parallels between objects mentioned in texts and those found in excavations. Even in periods when the languages of dispersed areas are related, as in the case of Indo-Aryan in northern India and its cognates in Anatolia and north-east Iran, the material culture of the societies speaking these languages is dissimilar.

The notion of an Aryan race was enhanced in the past by reference to the use of an Aryan language. The notion of an Aryan race has been discarded for at least the last fifty years. Language and race are distinctly different categories. It would be more correct to use the label of Indo-Aryan when referring to the language, and to use Aryan as *ārya*, as it was used in the past, to qualify those observing certain social and linguistic norms. The overlay of nineteenth century theories and the more generalised current debates has merely confused its usage. How and when the Indo-Aryan language became current in the upper Indus plain now requires investigation in the context of the linguistic forms that it has incorporated from other contemporary language groups. These are forms that exist only in Indo-Aryan and not in the other languages with which it was most closely associated in Iran and Anatolia (Emeneau 1954, Mehendale 1993). Had Indo-Aryan spread from the Punjab to Iran and Anatolia, then these borrowings should have been present in the language of the *Avesta* and the Mitanni-Hittite treaty (Mallory 1989). The spread of the Indo-Aryan language was a continuing process in Indian history. Within the subcontinent it was introduced for specific functions in addition to local languages. Where some of elements of the latter were inducted this could provide clues to the earlier process. The links and connections between societies across the Indo-Iranian borderlands could be examined through the evidence of artefacts travelling distances as well as linguistic changes among those using related languages.

This would suggest that we look for a graduated interaction over many centuries among the players who created these societies and cultures. There is little evidence for large scale violent conflict and constant warfare despite the Harappan cities being fortified. Why were elaborate fortifications necessary or was it assumed that they were somehow necessary to urbanism? The subsequent *Ṛgveda* describes inter-clan hostility, but on a small scale, sometimes among the *ārya* clans and sometimes between the *ārya*s and the *dāsa*s. *Ārya* priests on occasion performed rituals for *dāsa* chiefs even if their characteristic worship was different. The nature of these relationships could be fine-tuned. Texts on ritual exegesis associated with the *Ṛgveda* refer with respect even to those *brāhmaṇa*s who were the sons of *dāsa* women. This would query the simplistic understanding of caste as *varṇa* and applying the norms of the later *dharma-śāstra*s to earlier times. It would seem that the relationship was more ambivalent than has been granted so far (Kosambi 1950, Thapar 2000) The adoption of those outside the social pale into caste status also contradicts previous notions of caste exclusiveness *(Aitareya Brāhmaṇa* 7.18).

The centrality of the Vedic texts for later history has been largely treated as the continuity of ritual and belief systems. As religious texts they were highly respected in some circles and said to be divine revelations whereas others did not take them to be so. Eventually the popularity of Puranic Hinduism, which introduced rituals and belief systems from various other sources as well, superseded the centrality of the *Veda*s except among the topmost caste. For some philosophers and their large followings such as those of the Shramanic sects of Buddhists, Jainas, Ājīvikas, and such like, the *Veda*s had been one among the starting points of intellectual questioning, leading to a departure in beliefs and practice. This continued with lively confrontations, some compromises and some vitriolic exchange.

The evidence of social change in these texts has received less attention. Why some clans and castes come to dominate and others were subordinated in this period, have implications for social history. Hierarchies, differentiations and regulations are part of the social process in complex societies and evolve in localised exchanges. They cannot be explained away by resort to the presence of conquerors as they were in earlier studies, nor by the societies being described as uniformly and universally harmonious. Local hierarchies also undergo mutation. But when there is an insistence on making a system universal, such as the imposition of caste rules over extensive areas, then it has to be assumed that this reflects historical changes of a substantial kind, involving a diversity of groups not all of whom were in agreement. Where a range of groups have to be incorporated into positions of status, there ethnic origins may well have been set aside in favour of imposing a language and social norms. Language, inherited or learnt, would be a crucial indicator. Notions of what is indigenous and what is alien are neither permanent nor unchanging nor transparent. The identities of the indigenous and the alien constantly mutate throughout history and the mutation indicates a historical change.

The *Veda*s when treated as sources of history have to be subjected to the same analyses as all other sources. They are questioned in terms of who composed them, for what purpose, who's views do they reflect, and so on. It is significant that the hymns of the *Ṛgveda* as we have them now only in the recension of Śākalya were composed not all at the same time but over a few centuries. Therefore some change would be registered in the context of the early hymns as compared to the later. Social history would involve investigating the organisation of the various groups referred to as well as their rituals and their technologies and economies. A listing of items mentioned is not enough for it requires an assessment of the broader frameworks of social and economic functioning.

The application of the Aryan theory to Indian history began as an attempt to uncover the beginnings of Indian history, to explain the origins of Indian society and to establish what were thought to be the roots of Indian identity. This historical enterprise has on occasion become entangled with politics, both colonial and national, and possibly now, in the literally post-colonial formulation of both. The emphasis on defining a particular kind of Aryanism as foundational to Indian civilisation is not a radical indigenous interpretation of history as is claimed. It is a revival of certain trends in nineteenth century colonial historiography but now moulded by the more specific ideological concerns of contemporary time and place. In the past the theory has been used by many as an agency of empowerment and entitlement to include some and exclude others. This in itself cannot be curtailed since resort to history – particularly ancient history – has been part of the agenda of various nationalisms and imperialisms and continues to be so in some cases. Nevertheless, historians, archaeologists, specialists in linguistics and in other disciplines that bear on the subject, need to be constantly in a scholarly dialogue so as to assess the validity of the theories being suggested. Such verifications are also signposts for the interested general reader.

Bibliography

Bernal M., 1987, *Black Athena*, London.

Bryant E., 2001, *The Quest for the Origins of Vedic Culture*, Delhi.

Burrow T., 1973, 'The Proto-Indo-Aryans', *Journal of the Royal Asiatic Society*, 2, 123–40.

— —, 1965, *The Sanskrit Language*, London.

Caldwell R., 1856, *A Comparative Grammar of the Dravidian or South Indian Family of Languages*, London.

Darmesteter J., 1969 reprint, *The Zend-Avesta, Part I The Vendidad*, (Trans) Varanasi.

Das A.C., 1920, *Rigvedic India*, Calcutta.

Deshpande G. P., (ed.) 2002, *Selected Writings of Jotirao Phule*, New Delhi.

Deshpande M. M., 1979 'Genesis of Ṛgvedic Retroflexion', in M. M.Deshpande and P. Hook (eds.), *Aryan and Non-Aryan in India*, Ann Arbor.

Drew H., 1987, *India and the Romantic Imagination*, Delhi.

Elliot H. M. and Dowson J., 1996 reprint, *The History of India as Told by its Own Historians*, Varanasi.

Ellis P. W., 1816, 'Note to the Introduction', included in A.D. Campbell, *A Grammar of the Teloogoo Language*, quoted in part in T.Trautmann (ed.), 2005, *The Aryan Debate*, Delhi.

Emeneau M. B., 1954, 'Linguistic Prehistory of India', in *Proceedings of the American Philosophical Society*, 98, 282–92.

— —, 1974, 'Indian Linguistic Area Revisited', *International Journal of Dravidan Linguistics*, 3.1.93 ff.

Francfort H-P., 2005, 'La civilisation de l'Oxus et les Indo-Iraniens et Indo-Aryens', in G.Pussman et al. (eds), *Aryas, Aryens et Iraniens en Asie Centrale*, Paris, 253–328.

Fussman G., 2005, 'Entre fantasmes, science et politique: l'entrée des Aryas en Inde', in G. Fussman et al. (eds.), *Aryas, Aryens et Iraniens en Asie Centrale*, Paris, 197–232.

Gimbutas M., 1997, *The Kurgan Culture and the Indo-Europeanization of Europe*, Washington DC.

Golwalkar M. S., 1938, *We, Or Our Nationhood Defined*, Bombay.

Goodrick-Clarke N., 1992, *The Occult Roots of Nazism*, New York.

Hiebert P. T., 1994, *Origins of the Bronze Age Oasis Civilisation in Central Asia*, Cambridge, Mass.

Jacobi H.,1895, 'On the Date of the Rig-Veda', *Indian Antiquary, 23,* 154–9.

Jones W., 1788, 'Third Anniversary Discourse', *Asiatic Researches, 1,* 415–31.

Kellens J., 2005, 'Les *airiia* – ne sont pas des Aryas: ce sont deja des Iraniens', in G. Fussman et.al. (eds.), *Aryas, Aryens et Iraniens en Asie Centrale,* Paris, 233–252.

Kosambi D. D., 1950, 'On the Origin of Brahmin *Gotras*', reprinted in *Combined Methods in Indology and Other Writings,* 2002, Delhi, 98–166.

Kuiper F. B. J., 1991, *Aryans in the Ṛgveda,* Amsterdam.

Leopold J., 1974, 'British Applications of the Aryan Theory of Race to India, 1850–70', *The English Historical Review,* 89, 578-603; 'The Aryan Theory of Race in India 1870–1920, Nationalist and Internationalist Visions', *Indian Economic and Social History Review,* 1970, VII, 2, 271–298.

Leslie Willson A., 1964, *A Mythical Image: The Ideal of India in German Romanticism,* Durham.

Majumdar R. C., et al. (eds.), 1951, *The Vedic Age,* Bombay.

Mallory J.P., 1989, *In Search of the Indo-Europeans,* London.

Max Müller F., 1862, *Lectures on the Science of Language,* London.

— —, 1883, *India What Can it Teach Us?* London.

— —, 1884, *Biographical Essays,* Oxford. [This was an address delivered at the Bristol Museum On 27.9.1883, on the 50th anniversary of the Raja's death. See also, N. Mookerjee (ed.), *I Point to India,* Bombay 1970; 24–28.]

— —, 1888, *Biographies of Words and the Home of the Aryas,* Oxford.

— —, 1983 reprint, *Rigveda Samhita,* Varanasi

— —, 1898, *Auld Lang Syne,* London.

Mehendale M. A., 1993, 'Indo-Aryans, Indo-Iranians and Indo-Europeans', in S. B. Deo and S. Kamath (eds.), *The Aryan Problem,* Pune, 43–50.

Muir J., 1874–84, *Original Sanskrit Texts on the Origin and History of the People of India, Their Religions and Institutions,* London.

Nanda M., 2003, *Prophets Facing Backwards*, Delhi.

Narahari Achar B. N., 1999, 'On Exploring the Vedic Sky with Modern Computer Software', *Electronic Journal of Vedic Studies*, 5,2.

O'Hanlon, R., 1985, *Caste Conflict and Ideology*, Cambridge.

Omvedt G., 1991, *Jyotiba Phule: An Incomplete Renaissance*, Surat.

Parpola A., 1994, *Deciphering the Indus Script*, Cambridge.

Poliokov L., 1974, *The Aryan Myth*, New York.

Ramaswamy S., 1997, *Passions of the Tongue*, Berkeley.

Renfrew C., 1987, *Archaeology and Language*, Cambridge.

Risley H.H., 1908, *The People of India*, London.

Sarianidi V. I., 1999, 'Near Eastern Aryans in Central Asia', *The Journal of Indo-European Studies*, 27, 3-4, 295–326.

Savarkar V. D., 1922, *Hindutva, Who is a Hindu*, Bombay.

Schwab R., 1984 (trans.), *The Oriental Renaissance: Europe's Rediscovery of India and the East, 1680–1880*, New York.

Scott Littleton C., 1973, *The New Comparative Mythology: An Anthropological Assessment of the Theories of Georges Dumezil*, London.

Sen K. C., 1923, *Keshab Chunder Sen's Lectures in India*, Calcutta.

Stepan N., 1982, *The Idea of Race in Science: Great Britain 1800–1960*, London.

Taylor I., 1889, *The Origin of the Aryans: an Account of the Prehistoric Ethnology and Civilisation of Europe*, London.

Thapar R., 1969, 'Society in Ancient India: the Formative Period', reprinted in R.Thapar, *Cultural Pasts*, Delhi, 2000, 310–335.

— —, 1978 'Origin Myths and the Early Indian Historical Tradition', reprinted in R.Thapar, *Cultural Pasts*, Delhi 2000,754–781.

— —. 1983, 'The Archaeological Background to the Agnicayana Ritual', in F. Staal et al. (eds.), *Agni*, Berkeley, 1–40.

— —, 1984, *From Lineage to State*, Delhi.

——, 1989–91, 'Archaeology and Language at the Roots of Ancient India', *Journal of the Asiatic Society of Bombay,* 64–66 (n.s.), 249–268.

——, 2000, 'The *Ṛgveda*: Encapsulating Social Change', in K. N. Panikkar et al. (eds.), *The Making of History,* Delhi, 11–40.

Tilak B.G., 1893, *Orion or Researches into the Antiquity of the Vedas,* Poona.

——, 1903, *The Arctic Home in the Vedas,* Poona

Trautmann T. R., 1997, *Aryans and British India,* New Delhi.

—— (ed.), 2005, *The Aryan Debate,* Delhi.

Waddell L. A., 1925, *The Indo-Sumerian Seals Deciphered*, London.

Wilson J.,1877, *Indian Caste,* Bombay.

Witzel M., 1999, 'The Pleiades and the Bears Viewed from Inside the Vedic Texts', *Electronic Journal of Vedic Studies,* 5.2.

2.

Some Appropriations of the Theory of Aryan Race and the Beginnings of Indian History

The theory of Aryan race which sought to explain the beginnings of Indian history has been used in a variety of ways not only to structure knowledge about the past, but perhaps more directly to give legitimacy to the conflicts of the present. The theory has a genesis in colonial attempts to "discover" the Indian past, a discovery which is rooted in the colonial present. Indian concerns with trying to define an identity had to do with the colonial-nationalist relationship, as well as the relationship among Indians insisting on particular definitions. But the latter are also facets of the former since they would not have taken the form which they did outside of a colonial context. The two dichotomous interpretations discussed here – that of Phule and the Dalits, and that of the propagators of Hindutva – are both in dialogue with the colonial interpretations and with mainstream nationalism. The theory of Aryan race was not limited to historical reconstruction and is an example of how historical perceptions of the past can be related to conflictual situations of the present. Interpretations of the past have a bearing on the conduct of the conflict and the conflict in turn fashions the shape of what is viewed as the historical past.

Puranic lists of descent groups were the initial source material for the reconstruction of Indian history in the work of the early Orientalists. But the narrative changed with access to the Vedic corpus although the change was not immediate. William Jones' discussion of Sanskrit as a cognate of Greek and Latin led to his concern with a possible monogenesis of these languages, although his work preceded the adoption of the term 'Aryan'. This idea was further built upon in the studies of comparative philology at various European universities in the nineteenth century, drawing on the Vedic corpus which had recently become available. Monogenesis began to be applied to the speakers of these languages as well. These studies contributed to the notion of an Indo-European family of languages, descended from an ancestral language. This in turn required tracing the homeland of the ancestral language. By the latter half of the nineteenth century European scholarship was enthused with notions of Aryan origins and the search for the Aryan homeland, a search partly encouraged by German Romanticism and the view that India could be the cradle of the human race and civilsation.

Further studies in comparative philology coincided with the theories of the Comte de Gobineau searching for Aryan identities in Europe and warning against interbreeding. The classification of race, borrowed from biological studies, became influential as did the idea of the survival of the fittest as applied to human societies. The demonstrable impact of European colonialism also acted as a factor in changing the European view of itself and its origins. European origins were thus liberated from being tied down to Biblical history, and the latter was substituted with the theory of Aryan race. What has been described as race science was viewed as an accurate identification of human groups (Stepan). With the increasing success of imperialism and the view that Europe was the most advanced among the nations it was inevitable that the original Aryan would be relocated. By the end of the nineteenth century it was held that the Asian Aryans had their homeland in central Asia but that the European Aryans originated from the Nordic blondes of northern Europe (Taylor).

The theory of Aryan race came to be viewed as foundational to Indian history largely through what has been called the twinning of the theories of British Sanskritists and ethnographers (Trautmann), and the influential role of Max Müller. The texts which initially encouraged the idea were those constituting the Vedic corpus and in particular the *Ṛgveda*. Viewed as the most ancient literature and the key to Sanskrit and to Hindu civilisation, its references to the *ārya*s and to their hostility to the *dāsa*s were eagerly fitted into the theory that a clan of Aryans migrated from central Asia, invaded northern India enslaving the indigenous people, the *dāsa*s, and settled in India. The reference to *varṇa*/colour in the earliest text was easily read as skin pigmentation and seen as a graphic description of the fair-skinned Aryans conquering the dark-skinned aborigines.

The equation of language and race was instrumental in the formulating of the theory. Conquest introduced both the language Indo-Aryan and what has come to be called the distinctive Aryan civilisation. This became the opening narrative of Indian history. Racial separateness required a demarcation and the conquest became the mechanism by which caste came to be viewed as a form of racial segregation and central to Indian social institutions. Having given rise to the Aryan race, deriving from the Indo-Aryan language, the parallel to this theory was soon established in the notion of the Dravidian race based on the Dravidian languages, clearly formulated in the early grammars of Dravidian (e.g., Caldwell), and in the idea that Dravidian speakers are racially identifiable and native to India. In later years Max Müller stated that language and race were distinct categories but by then the equation had become an axiom and he himself frequently confused the two.

The equation has not only affected the understanding of the earliest past, in that the theory of Aryan race and the Aryan conquest of northern India became foundational to the beginnings of Indian history, but it has also been crucial to the conflicting views over Indian identity, sought to be established in more recent times. A range of social and political groups in India over the last century and a half have interpreted the theory variously and in order to support their own political and social aspirations. Aryanisation as a fact of the historical past is less contested, but what creates divergent views is the question of whether it was alien or indigenous.

The debate over how it was to be interpreted provides an insight into the political agendas of the groups who used it. These groups were involved in seeking identities from the past and in countering each other's claims to these identities as well as choosing a homeland and working out a national culture. The interpretation therefore hinged on specific ideological needs. Modifications in the interpretations suggest changes in the status and role of the groups identifying with it. The primary concern in establishing an Indian identity was the need to define the rightful inheritors of the land, all within the context of a gradually growing nationalism where the question of origins and affirmation of common descent were central to nation-building. Such a concern required legitimation from history, therefore the theory was of prime importance to the beginnings of Indian history. To this extent the theory played the same role in India as it did in Europe, servicing various European nationalisms. But in India it has been extended to discussions on a wider range such as the origins of caste and the constituents of culture. My attempt here is to focus on two important but contradictory views of the theory, both of which have resurfaced in post-colonial political developments in India.

The application of the theory to Vedic India was picked up in Christian missionary circles in India through the writings particularly of J. Muir and J. Wilson. They maintained that the lower castes were the indigenous inhabitants who had been conquered and oppressed by the *brāhmaṇa*s who represented the Aryan conquest. This provided one perspective for what was to eventually be labeled a Dalit view of the theory as expounded initially by Jyotiba Phule. Writing in the latter half of the nineteenth century, Phule argued that the original inhabitants of India were the *ādivāsī*s, among whom he includes the *śūdra*s and the *ati-śūdra*s and the untouchables, who were descendants of the heroic peoples led by the *daitya* king, Bali. Various such categories were included under the generic label of *kṣatriya*. The indigenous peoples under the leadership of Bali, fought the arrival of the *brāhmaṇa*s who for Phule represented the Aryan invasion, but were conquered and subordinated. Phule's "golden age" was the period prior to the Aryan invasion when *śūdra*s were cultivators, land-owners and warriors and had their own culture. The *brāhmaṇa*s are said to have deliberately invented caste so that the *śūdra*s would be kept permanently servile and divided among themselves. The *brāhmaṇa-śūdra* dichotomy reflected the demarcation as it existed in nineteenth century Maharashtra (O'Hanlon, Omvedt).

Phule draws on well-known myths to emphasise his point. Thus Bali is deprived of his territory by the deceit of Viṣṇu when he took the three steps as agreed upon but so expanded himself as to cover earth and heaven in the three. The loss of territory is also a loss of status. There is repeated reference to the *brāhmaṇa* Paraśurāma who annihilated the *kṣatriya*s twenty one times (Phule 1873). These legends are not found in the *Vedas* but in the *Mahābhārata* and the *Purāṇa*s (Adi-parvan, 98.1 ff.; *Bhāgavata* 9.15.13ff.), nevertheless Phule treats them as early history. The stories of the ten *avatāra*s were also woven in. The earliest Aryans came by sea in ships which were referred to as *matsya* and *kurma*; the later Aryans came by land and were associated with the *varāha*, *narasiṃha* and *vāmana avatāra*s conquering and killing the *kṣatriyas*.

Phule was not merely concerned with the indigenous origins of the lower castes but was also a social reformer working towards educating *śūdra*s and women with the intention of providing them with a sense of relative independence. The founding of the Satyashodhak Samaj was intended to encourage an awareness of their rights among the lower castes. In the colonial-nationalist divide his views were not entirely supportive of either. British administration was seen as less severe than the previous Peshwa regime which had oppressed the tax-paying lower castes and supported the upper caste money-lenders. Phule's battle was also part of the confrontations which were developing between the *brāhmaṇa*s seen as the ex-Peshwas and the Marathas and Kunbis with the latter aspiring to power at different levels in association with the changes brought about by colonial administration.

In this version, the Aryan invasion and its consequences was a necessary event and has now become an essential part of the Dalit version of Indian history. It was to influence a variety of non-Brahmin movements in different parts of the peninsula. The dichotomy between Brahmin and non-Brahmin was seen to provide a rational explanation for the pattern of history and for the suppression of the non-*brāhmaṇa* by the *brāhmaṇa*. This dichotomy was easily slotted into the linguistic division of the Aryan and Dravidian languages where the *brāhmaṇa*s were seen as Sanskrit educated Aryans and the other castes using Dravidian languages as the non-Aryans. The input of language demarcation was perhaps one reason for the non-Brahmin movement being more influential in peninsular India than elsewhere. The self-perception of Dravidian speakers was tied to the anti-Brahmin movement symbolizing the rejection of Aryan dominance. The political importance of this interpretation lay in the idea that true nationalism required giving power to the original inhabitants of the land. Phule used the theory to oppose *brāhmaṇa* domination, arguing that they were alien Aryans and therefore not the rightful inheritors of the land, the latter being the lower castes. Phule radicalized the theory in order to use it in his campaign against *brāhmaṇa* domination. The generic label of *kṣatriya* which Phule gave to non-*brāhmaṇa*s, encouraged claims to upward mobility among certain lower castes.

Interestingly, the confrontation from the brahmanical side arises from, among others, the views of some Chitpavan *brāhmaṇa*s and some other *brāhmaṇa*s based in Maharashtra. The Chitpavan *brāhmaṇa*s had been privileged as Peshwas but were no longer so, leading to both discontent and attempts to negotiate concessions from the colonial administration. These groups did not debate the issue of caste status with the followers of Phule but preferred to work out their own interpretation of the Aryan theory, contradicting that of Phule. This also became central in the Hindutva version.

A move in this direction can be seen earlier in the writings of the Theosophists and particularly those of Col. Olcott in the late nineteenth century. Olcott maintained that *āryavarta* was the cradle of civilisation and the Aryans were a race indigenous to northern India, their literature being the source of all philosophy and religion. Many Theosophists felt that Hinduism came closest to being a universal religion, which was much sought after at the time, and that Hindu practice and the Aryan heritage should be conserved even though it meant retaining caste hierarchies. Above all, the Aryan was identified with the Hindu. The views of Col. Olcott and Annie Besant in particular in this regard, were eagerly endorsed by many Hindus who believed in their veracity as coming from British sympathisers with what was now regarded as a Hindu 'renaissance'. They could well have influenced Hindutva thinking.

The Hindutva version, formulated in the 1920s, glossed over the question of an invasion when referring to the Aryans as having settled in northern India but emphasised their racial distinctiveness and their role as the progenitors of the Hindus. This facilitated the endorsing of the indigenous origins of the Aryans which followed closely as a theory, as did the insistence that Sanskrit was an indigenous language. Living in the Sindhu/Indus plain welded them into a nation and gave them the name of Hindu, derived from Sindhu. There was an insistence on a homeland within the Indian sub-continent. Since India was the homeland of the Aryans, Aryan civilisation travelled from India to the west. All Hindus are members of the Aryan race, and therefore are not aliens. Hindus are united by the bonds of common blood, the blood of the mighty race, incorporated with and descended from the Vedic forefathers (Savarkar 68). The Race-Spirit of the Hindus did not die out and enabled the Hindus to defend themselves against "the murdering hordes of mussalman freebooters" (Golwalker 10). Equally clear is the listing of common cultural characteristics. The constituents of a nation are, the territory hereditarily occupied, race, religion and culture which create the Race-Spirit, and language (Golwalkar 18 ff; 28 ff;). Those who do not belong to the Hindu nation cannot live in India except as foreigners unless they agree to be 'naturalised', namely, discard their previous religion, culture and language.

This view is clear about what constitutes the Indian/Hindu identity. Savarkar maintained that an Indian/Hindu is one for whom India is his *pitṛbhūmi* and his *puṇyabhūmi,* the land of his ancestors and the land of his religion. This definition of the Indian/Hindu and the Hindu Arya effectively cut out the Muslims and the Christians which was intentional according to the text, and to this was also added the Communists! There is therefore a confusion of categories – race, religion and ideology. The link between these views and the beginnings of Indian history is that they have become influential in popular versions of history, and the demands of political ideology have led to attempts to change school text-books in order to give the Hindutva interpretation.

The concept of the Hindu Arya created problems in relation to what colonial administration called Scheduled Castes. Whether these groups constituted Hindu Aryas or not was debated among caste Hindus. The more orthodox supporters of Hindutva were for excluding them, but when the game of numbers was seen as important to democratic institutions, there was a move to incorporate the Scheduled Castes as Hindus and thus swell the numbers of the Hindus. Reference was made by some to the common blood of all Hindus from the *brāhmaṇa* to the *Cāṇḍāla* (Savarkar 89). But the issue remains somewhat confused in the Hindutva version because Golwalkar returns to the concept of the Race-Spirit (39-40) inspired by Nazi Germany, although his actual intention was the separating of Hindus and Muslims. Common blood and the purity of race allowed for a separate Hindu identity. But the problem remained, for if the Aryans incorporated the non-Aryans then it could be argued that this had interfered with racial purity.

The theory had to be changed from that of Phule in order to claim the antiquity and continuity of the Hindu *Rāṣṭra* and to provide a different identity to the Hindu, distinct from Indians following other religions. Phule saw the theory of Aryan race as an attempt by the upper castes to consolidate power and endorse hierarchy through insisting on inequality in relation to supposed origins. For him, the Aryan *brāhmaṇa* was 'the Other'. In the Hindutva version it is not the Aryan who is 'the Other', but the non-Hindu. This is a significant shift from caste to religion. But neither of these two versions was initially hegemonic.

There was a mainstream version which, deriving from Max Müller, was acceptable to upper-caste middle-class Hindus. Max Müller was seen as sympathetic to Indian civilisation which for him was essentially Hindu. This is the version with which we are all familiar from earlier histories of India. It is stated that there was an Aryan invasion and that the Aryans, speaking Indo-Aryan or Vedic Sanskrit, conquered the indigenous population, culturally and racially distinct from the Aryan. Support for this theory took some rather emphatic forms. Max Müller and Muir had maintained that upper caste Hindus were the biological, lineal descendants of the Aryans. The claim to kinship ties with the British based on the Aryan connection became an attempt at self-promotion by upper caste Hindus (Keshub Chunder Sen).

Colonial historians found the theory attractive because it provided a parallel to the British conquest of India and the introduction of western civilization through this process, a view which is partially responsible for the rejection of the Aryans being other than indigenous in some extreme nationalist opinion. The parallel would endorse the idea that the progress of India was dependent on the return of the Aryan in the guise of the British. The explanation of caste as racial segregation made caste more comprehensible and easier to manage than the more complex theories of kinship, occupation and rules of purity and pollution. Indian history was also brought into the current European discourse on race.

Some nationalist opinion had a different reading. Dayanand Saraswati propagated a return to the *Veda*s, the source of Indian civilization, and Sanskrit, the mother tongue of all languages, thus implicitly emphasizing the status of the *brāhmaṇa*. The purity of Sanskrit was insisted upon and has contributed to a suspicion of modern linguistics which does not endorse this purity. B. G. Tilak visualised a long march from the Arctic lands which he placed at the time of the receding Ice Ages. Tilak had little time for the views of Phule. For him the coming of the Aryans was a positive development in Indian history. He took the date of the *Ṛgveda* back to 4500 BC largely on the basis of what he computed as evidence from the position of the constellations. He placed the homeland in the Arctic and posited two groups of Aryans who migrated away from the homeland: the European Aryans who had settled in northern Europe but had soon relapsed into barbarism, and those who finally arrived in India and came to be seen as the Indian Aryans who retained their cultural superiority and conquered the non-Aryans. Indian civilization continued as a timeless civilization going back to the original Aryans. Tilak's views created some problem for the supporters of the Hindutva theory since he was arguing for an Arctic homeland and the Aryans as alien conquerors. This was too great a parallel to what the Hindutva ideology was battling against – the Muslims as alien conquerors pouring in from the north-west. The only way around was a reformulation stating that the Aryans did inhabit the area of the north pole but in those early days the north pole was located in present day Bihar and Orissa (Golwalkar 8).

In these cases the theory was closely tied to nationalism and was used to strengthen the status of the upper castes from which there came the new middle-class professionals. There was now an inching towards a class utilization of the theory to explain the superiority of those belonging to the emergent middle-class. The caste/class agenda of these readings seems to be so essential that there is little or no attempt to even dismiss Phule's reading. Implicit in much of the wider discussion was that caste was a form of racial segregation (Risley) and a scientific way of organizing society.

Whereas Phule was less interested in race and concentrated on caste, in the Hindutva version racial identity and nationalism are collapsed. There is a swing therefore from concerns of caste to those of purity of blood and to religious identities. The concept of race was alien, hence the translation of the word inappropriately as *jāti*. The choice was probably determined by the circular argument that caste was racial segregation. To assume that this was a correct translation because *jāti* can mean 'species', is problematic. Although the word *jāti* is linked to birth, the identification of *jātis* is also drawn from a variety of social and religious activities and these continually change the boundaries of *jāti* identity. The recognition of inter-breeding among *jāti*s would also militate against its being defined as race, as does the fact that *jāti*s are constantly incorporating and creating new *jāti*s. Caste had been frequently contested in history but with other markers such as language, occupation, and sect, and had been continually redefined. But when race was introduced into this contestation it was projected as the most 'scientific' of the markers.

The history of social change within a caste-based society was given little attention by earlier historians, many of whom were content to project the frozen nature of caste. With language and caste both being identified as racial identities, cultural history was frequently explained in terms of the spread of the Aryan race and its culture, monitored by the presence of Brahmanical belief and practice. A gradual departure from this general assessment of the impact of the Aryans was the realization by culture historians, sociologists and anthropologists, and some studying Indian religion, that there was more than upper caste Aryanism in the making of Indian history and civilization (Bose, Ghurye, Karve). This was also an attempt to broaden the base of nationalist inclusive history.

The variant interpretations of the Aryan theory illustrate its role in the political agendas of various social groups and the nature of the contestation between these groups. It reflects therefore what has been called the organizing capacity of intellectual rationalizations in the form of theories of fictive ethnicity (Balibar and Wallerstein). Appeal to a seemingly scientific explanation of biological heredity is made to coincide with racial categories. It provides nationalist myths of selective linear history in which the genetic descent of a 'nation' is sought to be traced and authority comes naturally to those of the upper castes or of the dominant religion; or alternatively a demand is made for the restitution of the rights of those who see themselves as having been denied their claims to being the inheritors of the land. Racism presupposes a fear of bastardization and underlines separateness. It is at the same time intelligible to large numbers and touches on commonly felt insecurities. It has also endorsed sub-nationalist identity myths, again based on the equation of language with race.

For a few decades the theory received less attention, perhaps because the earlier linear historical narrative had been shaken up by the newly discovered archaeological evidence of the Indus civilization. This evidence had to be incorporated into the theory, and accommodated to the evidence of the Vedic corpus, creating a new problem since the two sources were not compatible. Indo-European language studies were more generally beginning to introduce archaeological evidence in the reconstruction of societies said to be using Indo-European languages. The discovery of the Indus civilization raised pertinent questions regarding the Aryan beginnings of Indian history. There was of course the inevitable search for the Aryans in archaeological evidence and for a while every new archaeological culture dating to a period between 3000–1000 BC tended to be labeled as 'Aryan'. In a sense, the fashion had been set by Gordon Childe, but without his caveats it became a wild goose chase. Cautioning against equating archaeological cultures with languages in the absence of a deciphered script, was generally dismissed.

The foremost of the obstacles posed by the archaeological data was the existence of the urban, Harappan civilization which was prior to the Vedic sources and very different in culture from the Vedic; and equally important, what appeared to be the absence of evidence of any large scale invasion during this period. Such a change in evidence was problematic for all the accepted theories.

The development of Harappan urban centres in northern and western India observed a similarity of cultural form which is distinctively different from the diversity of pre-Harappan cultures each limited to a particular region (Allchin, Chakrabarti). The

Harappan cities used these as a base although the process of urbanization seems to have had its genesis in the Indus plain itself in about 2600 BC. Late Harappan cities decline by the early second millennium BC, but some of the smaller settlements continue and then peter out or else are mutated through contact with other locally evolved cultures. These sometimes provide periods of over lap between the Late Harappan and the subsequent culture, such as the Black-and-Red Ware in Gujarat and at a few sites of the Painted Grey Ware in the Punjab. Some continuities, albeit limited, can therefore be posited between the Harappan and post-Harappan cultures.

New cultures emerge at various places by the end of the second millennium as in the Swat valley, Baluchistan, Gujarat, Punjab, Rajasthan and the Ganga valley, but have their own individual and recognizably different characteristics. There is more than a hint of continuing contacts across the Indo-Iranian borderlands. The question then is whether the new items which surface as a result of these contacts can be linked to the presence of Indo-Aryan speakers.

The questioning of the theory of an Aryan invasion arose from the paucity of archaeological evidence suggesting such an invasion. There is occasional evidence of what appears to be the destruction of a site, sometimes by burning. Skirmishes and local conflicts can be expected. But there is no replacement on a large scale of local cultures by an intruding culture or the destruction of sites systematically over a sizable area.

The questioning of the theory of Aryan invasion has been received in different ways by the supporters of the Dalit and the Hindutva versions of the beginnings of Indian history. The invasion hypothesis was foundational to the Dalit version, therefore there continues to be an insistence on a large-scale Aryan invasion irrespective of the evidence for it. The Indus civilisation is now associated with Phule's pre-Aryan 'golden age' and the archaeology of the cities is used to emphasise the superiority of the earlier culture over the Vedic upper caste culture. The more recent label of Dalit Bahujan has been introduced into the narrative to make it more appropriate to the historical reconstruction which would endorse the claims of the Dalits and the lower castes to political status. Indra is said to have led the Aryans who exterminated the Adi-Dravidians who were also the Adi-Dalit Bahujanas, then living in the Indus plain (Ilaiah 73ff.). Viṣṇu was specially incarnated to kill Bali, the Dalit Bahujana *cakravarti,* because Bali did not believe in Hindu Brahmanism and worked to establish a casteless society.

The Hindutva version claims to have been vindicated if the evidence for an invasion is slight or absent, for now it can be more emphatically said that the Hindu Arya and Brahmanism were indigenous to India (Deo and Kamath, Frawley). But this also requires that the argument be taken further. Therefore the large amount of archaeological data prior to the generally accepted date of the *Veda*s is sought to be incorporated into the story by insisting that the Harappa culture is the archaeological counterpart to the *Ṛgveda,* the date of which would go back to the fourth millennium BC. The *Veda*s and the Aryans therefore, remain foundational to the beginnings of Indian history. Archaeological cultures are sought to be explained in terms of Vedic texts and the historicity of the texts is sought to be established by equating them with archaeological cultures. Inevitably it is claimed that the Harappa script has been deciphered and reads as a form of early Sanskrit. The Aryans remain distinctive, superior, indigenous and the progenitors of an Indian/Hindu civilization. The Hindu Aryas can be easily differentiated from non-Hindu foreigners and have an even longer and stronger lineal descent than before.

Archaeologists supporting this view maintain that the Indus civilisation should be renamed the Indus-Sarasavati civilization. This is on the basis of a large number of pre- and Mature Harappan sites clustered in Cholistan in the third millennium BC. This part of the Hakra river was identified by some with the Sarasvatī as mentioned in the *Ṛgveda* (S. P. Gupta, V. N. Misra). The argument derives from a mechanical counting of sites irrespective of their size or significance along the now dry Hakra, and from the location in the same area of a large Harappan mound of an urban centre as yet unexcavated. Changing the name attempts to capture the Indus Civilization for Hindu India. It also reflects the priority given to territory as the basis of the Hindu Arya identity where it reached out to the sub-continent and most particularly to the northwest. The original homeland – Sindhusthan, or the Indus plain – being now in Pakistan, makes that the area for the foundational civilization. That the insistence is on calling it Indus-Sarasvatī rather than the geographically more appropriate Indus-Hakra, should the contribution of the Hakra valley be regarded as necessary, also points to the intention in changing the name.

Not surprisingly these various Hindutva versions either deny the validity of the linguistic analyses or else ignore them. Linguistic analyses of Vedic Sanskrit, establishing it as part of the wider Indo-European family with cognates in Old Iranian grew out of studies in comparative philology. Subsequent to this, Grierson's *Linguistic Survey of India* dominated the study of Indian languages, and the history of language in India was seen largely in terms of the spread of Indo-Aryan. Now it is being argued that there are non-Aryan linguistic components in Indo-Aryan even as early as the *Ṛgveda* (Kuiper, Emeneau, Burrow 1965). One view describes some elements as linguistic convergence (Hock). This has implications for equating the identity of blood and language among Vedic Aryans.

The isolated occurrence of Proto-Indo-Aryan with no intervening evidence from places located between northern Mesopotamia and northern India, remains unexplained. Attempts to circumvent this problem result in having to maintain that Proto-

Indo-Aryan is later than Vedic Sanskrit and therefore derived from the latter and has to be seen as pure Sanskrit, and is an example of the spread of Indo-Aryan from an Indian homeland: a view which specialists in linguistics would find unacceptable. Even archaeology does not provide any similarities in the material cultures of northern Mesopotamia in the second millennium BC and those of India, nor for that matter any comparable changes in the northern Mesopotamian cultures at that time. That Vedic Sanskrit preceded Proto-Indo-Aryan would be necessary if the *Ṛgveda* is dated to 4500 BC rather than to the later and preferred date of most Indologists, namely, c. 1500 BC. But since Proto-Indo-Aryan is firmly dated to the mid-second millennium BC, Vedic Sanskrit cannot be much earlier. A more plausible explanation suggests that Proto-Indo-Aryan speakers from northern Iran branched off, with some migrating to northern Mesopotamia and others to Iran and finally to northern India (Burrow 1973). There may well have been a period of an original Indo-Iranian language which would explain the closeness in the language of the *Gāthā*s and the *Ṛgveda,* subsequent to which the Indo-Aryan speakers migrated to India.

The monitoring of non-Aryan in Vedic Sanskrit provides an interesting pattern. Non-Aryan is present in the *Ṛgveda* but makes a stronger presence with the shift in geographical location from the Punjab to the Ganga valley, a shift which is evident from the distribution of the dialects of Indo-Aryan in the Vedic corpus (Witzel) and the occasional reference in the *Veda*s to migrations eastwards. The archaeological picture of the Ganga valley indicates that it was peopled with earlier settlements with whom those coming from the Indo-Gangetic watershed would have had to make adjustments. A case in point is the spread of the Painted Grey Ware culture into the *doāb* where it occupied sites close to those of the earlier Ochre Colour Pottery culture and those of the Black-and-Red Ware cultures (Roy T. N.). Any single one of these cultures need not be identified with 'the Aryans', but there is an interaction between these cultures which may be reflected in the language of the Indo-Aryan speakers as recorded in the later Vedic corpus. Not only has a borrowing of some vocabulary been suggested, as for example words relating to agricultural processes, but also the currency of morphological and phonetic forms and syntax from Proto-Dravidian and Austro-Asiatic. This was a mixing of two distinctive language systems, the agglutinative Proto-Dravidian and the inflectional Indo-Aryan. This has reinforced the theory that the speakers of Indo-Aryan migrated into northern India from north-eastern Iran and Afghanistan and settled among non-Aryan speakers, with possibly a long-period of bilingualism which accounts for the presence of non-Aryan in Vedic Sanskrit (Emeneau). Differences in Vedic dialects and the emergence of a variety of Prākrits by the middle of the first millennium would also suggest a mingling of the speakers of various languages, quite apart from the changes resulting from the natural evolution of the language.

From the Hindutva perspective, archaeology is now viewed as important to the identity of the Aryans, but less so linguistics. The past is thought to be out there, waiting to be discovered. Archaeology provides tangible data and greater chronological precision than the literary source, but it poses other problems. In stating that the Harappans were Vedic Aryans, the earlier priority given to the Vedic corpus is tied into archaeological data even if it means some doubtful reading of the *Ṛgveda* or of the interpretations of archaeological artefacts. The evidence from linguistic data supports the early form of Indo-Aryan having migrated from across the borderlands, therefore those favouring the indigenous origins of Indo-Aryan prefer to ignore the linguistic evidence. Denying or under-emphasising this evidence relates not only to the controversy over whether Indo-Aryan was indigenous but to the far more significant questions of the processes of historical change in the first millennium BC.

The replacing of invasion by migration raises another set of questions. These would require a change in perspective among mainstream historians as well as among those using the theory as political ideology. Did the *ārya*s decimate the *dāsa*s and was the differentiation one of skin colour?

The questioning of the racial distinction and of an Aryan invasion, requires a reorientation in the interpreting of the history of these times. If Aryan is a language label and has no racial connotation then the historian has to explain how the language entered India and came to be established as the language of the elite. Languages come with people but those that speak the same language need not be racially the same. The spread of a language does not have to be linked to overwhelming numbers of people. The process of language change can be achieved if other factors relating to the historical context encourage it. If there is an insistence that Indo-Aryan evolved within India and without any contact with other regions, then its linguistic prehistory will have to be demonstrated to show the process of evolution in isolation to the point where it becomes Vedic Sanskrit.

Archaeology, in the absence of inscriptions, cannot provide the evidence for a language or for a change of language. But it can provide the evidence for the functioning of various societies, contacts between societies and a broad delineation of the social and economic system. It can be suggested on the basis of what seems to have been much coming and going across the Indo-Iranian borderlands, judging by the presence of artefacts in different areas, that there may have been small-scale migrations motivated by pastoralism and incipient trade, both of which were well-established activities from earlier Harappan times. Migrations and the inter-change of language in these areas has been a constant feature of its history over the millennia. In the course of such movements it is possible that pastoral clans with a mobile segment using horses, began to negotiate alliances with the settlements which had survived the economic collapse of the Harappan system. In a period of predators, protectors would have the advantage. This advantage did not depend solely on conquest or coercive dominance. It would have involved skirmishes and raids of the kind which are referred to in the *Ṛgveda* as also negotiations and alliances and a slow process of interaction with the existing populations. The latter may have resulted in groups which fissioned off and their culture would be far more mixed and distanced from the original migrants. Such processes take their own time and it is not surprising that the change in geographical location and the linguistic changes from the *Ṛgveda* to the later Vedic corpus took more than half a millennium and probably longer. The conflicts referred to in the Vedic corpus can better be viewed from a historical perspective as between various social groups, pastoralists and peasants. But even these were not clearly demarcated and there were many over-lapping forms.

Language reflects vertical and horizontal relationships between groups, and particular groups come to be associated with particular languages. Historically this becomes a study of incorporation and negotiation where oppression and intolerance are not negated but their authors have to be identified within the society rather than as racial outsiders. Such an approach therefore does away with the simplistic explanation of caste being the result of a conquest and recognition of racial separateness, or the denial of oppression through insisting that the population had an unchanging identity. The *āryas* emerge not as a distinctive people, physically different from others and known as 'the Aryans' but as persons of status in many of the societies of that time (Burrow 1959). Nor were the differentiations between *ārya*s and *dāsa*s based on the idea that there was a permanent differentiation between the two in their ways of living, economies, custom, ritual, languages. The components of identities constantly change over time. Socio-economic differences reflected in the *Ṛgveda* and the *Brāhmaṇa*s require historical explanations. Both the Dalit and the Hindutva perspective would have problems with this approach and would therefore wish to maintain their original explanations.

It is paradoxical that the early Indian texts which claim to narrate the Indian past do not situate the beginning in anything which resembles the conquest of the area nor do they refer to the *ārya*s as being the founders of Indian culture. Thus the *vaṃśānucarita* section of the *Viṣṇu Purāṇa* starts the narrative with the reign of the seven Manus which is followed by a deluge after which the two main descent groups – the Sūryavaṃśa and the Candravaṃśa – are established and there are lengthy lists of *kṣatriya rājā*s. The war at Kurukṣetra virtually marks the termination of this list and the history of the subsequent period is narrated in the form of dynasties which continue until the time of the Guptas. As in many traditional perceptions of the past a relatively unbroken, lineal narrative is sought.

The subject of Aryanism and the beginnings of Indian history remains a complex problem because it still carries, at the popular level, the baggage of nineteenth century European preconceptions, even if in the European context it has now been rejected as a nineteenth century myth (Poliakov, Leach). It has overwhelmed Indian history whereas actually it is not so central. It is now less central to a nationalist reconstruction of the past, although the Hindutva version claims to derive from a nationalist cause and accuses those who disagree of being anti-national. But its real function is political in that it is used to separate the supposedly indigenous Hindu Arya from the alien, the Muslim and the Christian; or the indigenous lower castes from the alien upper castes. It is thus a mechanism used in the present day confrontation between social groups. The crux of the debate is the crisis of identity and status in the claims to political and social power and a contestation over what is viewed as alternative forms of national culture and ethnic homogeneity.

References

Allchin F. R.(ed.), *The Archaeology of Early Historic South Asia,* Cambridge 1995.

Balibar E. and Wallerstein I., *Race, Nation, Class,* London 1991.

Bose N. K., 'Caste in India', *Man in India,* 1951, 31, 3-4, pp. 107-23.

Bunow T., 'Iranian *ārya* and *dāha*', *Transactions of the Philological Society,* 1959, p. 71 ff.

— —, *The Sanskrit Language,* London 1965.

— —, 'The Proto-Indo-Aryans', *Journal of the Royal Asiatic Society,* 1973, 2, pp. 123-40.

Caldwell R., *A Comparative Grammar of the Dravidian or South Indian Family of Languages*, London 1856.

Chakrabarti D. K., *The Archaeology of Ancient Indian Cities,* Delhi 1995.

Deo S. B. and Kamath S. (eds.), *The Aryan Problem,* Pune 1993.

Emeneau B. M., 'Indian Linguistic Area Revisited', *International Journal of Dravidian Linguistics,* 1974, 3, 1, p. 93 ff.

Frawley D., *The Myth of the Aryan Invasion of India,* New Delhi 1994.

Ghurye G. S., *Vedic India,* Delhi 1979.

Golwalkar M. S., *We or Our Nationhood Defined,* Bombay 1938.

Gordon Childe V. G., *New Light on the Most Ancient East,* London 1934.

— —, *The Aryans,* London 1926.

Gupta S. P., 'Longer Chronology of the Indus Sarasvati Civilisation', *Puratattva,* 1992-93, 23, pp. 21-29.

Hock H. H., 'Subversion or Convergence? The Issue of Pre- Vedic Retroflexion Re-examined', in *Studies in the Linguistic Sciences,* 1993, 23, 2, 74-109.

Ilaiah K., *Why I am not a Hindu,* Calcutta 1996.

Karve I., *Kinship Organisation in India,* Bombay 1961.

Kuiper F. B. J., *Aryans in the Ṛgveda,* Amsterdam 1991.

Leach E., 'Aryan Invasions over four Millennia', in E. Ohnuki-Tierney (ed.), *Culture Through Time,* Stanford 1990.

Mallory J. P., *In Search of the Indo-European,* London 1989.

Misra V. N., 'Indus Civilisation and the Ṛgvedic Sarasvati', in A. Parpola et al. *South Asian Archaeology* 1993, Vol. II, Helsinki 1994.

Muir J., *Original Sanskrit Texts,* London 1858–63.

Max Müller F., *Lectures on the Science of Language,* Oxford 1862.

——, *India, What Can it Teach Us?* Oxford 1883.

——, *Chips from a German Workshop,* Oxford 1884.

——, *Biographical Essays,* Oxford 1884.

——, *Biographies of Words and the Home of the Aryas,* Oxford 1888.

——, (ed.), *Rig-veda-Saṃhitā,* Varanasi 1983 (reprint).

O'Hanlon R., *Caste Conflict and Ideology,* Cambridge 1985.

Omvedt G., *Jyotiba Phule : an Incomplete Renaissance,* Surat 1991.

Phule J., *Gulamgiri*, 187 3, Bombay 1986 (tr). See also, G. P. Deshpande (ed.), *Selected Works of Jyotirao Phule*, Delhi 2002, pp. 23–100.

Poliokov L., *The Aryan Myth,* New York 1974.

Rajaram N. S., 'Vedic and Harappan Culture: New Findings', *Puratattva,* 1993-94, 24, pp.1-11.

——, *The Politics of History: Aryan Invasion theory and the Subversion of Scholarship,* New Delhi 1995.

Ratnagar S., *Encounters, The Westerly Trade of the Harappan Civilisation,* Delhi 1981.

Risley H., *The People of India,* London 1908.

Roy T. N., *The Ganges Civilisation,* New Delhi 1983.

Savarkar V. D., *Hindutva : who is a Hindu,* distributed 1922, published Poona 1969.

Sen K. C., *Keshab Chander Sen's Lectures in India,* Calcutta. p. 323.

Stepan N., *The Idea of Race in Science: Great Britain 1800-1960,* London 1982.

Taylor I., *The Origin of the Aryans,* London 1892 (2nd ed.).

Tilak B. G., *Orion or Researches into the Antiquity of the Vedas,* Poona 1893.

— —, *The Arctic Home in the Vedas,* Poona 1903.

Trautmann T., *Aryans and British India,* (forthcoming).

Wilson J., *Indian Caste,* Bombay 1877.

Witzel M., 'Tracing the Vedic Dialects', in C.Caillat (ed.), *Dialectes dans les Litteratures Indo-Aryennes,* Paris 1989, p. 97 ff.

3.

Exploring Societies in the Early Past

I would like to take as my theme an exploration in the study of societies in ancient India and to deal with the period from *circa* 2500 BC to 500 BC in northern India, treating it principally as an occasion to demonstrate what I mean by a reorientation of perspectives.

The beginnings of Indian history have been projected for decades now in the invasion of northern India by the Aryans and the establishment of Aryan culture as a result of this conquest. The projection was that of a racially superior people. The study of both the Sanskrit texts and of ethnology went into the making of this theory.[1] Let me say at the outset that I am not concerned with 'the Aryan problem' *per se* in this Address. It is perhaps the biggest red herring that was dragged across the path of historians of India.[2] What I am concerned with is the need to understand the evolution of society at this time. This is a crucial period not only because a formative pattern of Indian culture took shape, but also because it provides clues to a more analytical understanding of subsequent periods of Indian history. The most serious of the many claims to have deciphered the Harappa script, in terms of the methodology used and the discussion it has provoked, has been that of the scholars who have read the script as proto-Dravidian.[3] An interesting facet of the controversy has been the vehemence of the loyalty to the respective Indo-Aryan and Dravidian language groups, with undertones almost of an Aryan and a Dravidian nationalism! This, in spite of the fact that specialists in both languages have for many years been suggesting that although linguistically distinct, at the cultural level at least this dichotomy is false.[4]

Our starting point could be the fact that we have two types of evidence, archaeological and literary. The literary sources are well-known and comprise the corpus of Vedic literature. The archaeological evidence consists of a number of cultures, most of them seemingly disparate. The earliest are the pre-Harappan cultures; the Sothi culture[5] of the Hakra valley and northern Rajasthan and the Chalcolithic village sites of Baluchistan and Sind. These were the precursors of the Harappa culture (c. 2600–1750 BC) and some culminated in Harappan settlements.[6] Of the post-Harappan cultures there is evidence from both the Indus and Ganga valleys. In northern Punjab the Gandhara Grave culture[7] (c. 1200–500 BC), using a red ware and a plain grey ware, shows evidence of copper in the early stages and later an iron technology, and contacts with Iran and central Asia. The Banas culture of southern Rajasthan (c. 2000–1200 BC, with possible extensions in the Ganga valley coming down to 800 BC) with its characteristic white-painted Black-and-Red pottery and its probable internalizing of certain Harappan forms, possibly acted as a bridge between the Late Harappan and post-Harappan cultures.[8] In the upper Ganga valley the earliest remains belong to the culture represented by the Ochre Colour Pottery which is post-Harappan in time range (c. 1400–1200). This has been associated sometimes with the Copper Hoard Culture[9] found both in the Doāb and in southern Bihar, and whose authors were perhaps the Munda speaking peoples. At some sites in Bihar there is evidence of the Black-and-Red ware (occasionally white-painted and similar to that of the Banas Culture) forming the earliest level. In parts of the Doāb it succeeds the Ochre Colour Pottery and precedes the predominant culture of the region. The latter is the Painted Grey Ware[10] (*c*. 1100–400) an initially agrarian culture familiar with iron technology and the horse. Finally, the Northern Black Polished Ware culture (c. 600–100) is associated with urbanization in the Ganga valley.

The archaeological picture therefore shows a large variety of cultures, none of which can be identified as specifically Aryan.[11] Nor does the evidence suggest that there was a single dominating culture or culture trait that slowly spread throughout northern India bringing the various diverse cultures into its fold, which is what one would expect if the popular notion of the spread of Aryan culture be accepted. In comparing the Indian and west Asian material there is again little consistent evidence of a dominant culture recognisably coming from west Asia to India, or for that matter going from India to west Asia, though there are certain similarities of techniques, such as the socketed axe and in ceramics. This would suggest migrants carrying aspects of technology and probably their language.

In comparing literary and archaeological evidence it is important to determine the nature of the society concerned. In the case of the *Ṛgveda* the geographical focus is that of the *sapta sindhavaḥ* from the Kabul river to what in the *Ṛgveda* is called the Sarasvatī river.[12] Ṛgvedic society is essentially a pre-urban society with a copper and possibly iron technology.[13] It evolves from nomadic pastoralism dependent on cattle to an agrarian form with more settled communities. Barley (*yava*) appears to have been the staple food. There is a strong sense of clan identity and the basic social unit is the patriarchal family. Close linguistic connections with Iran are evident. The important deities are Indra, Mitra, Varuṇa, Savitṛ, Soma and Agni. There is a distinct feeling of cultural exclusiveness and separation from some local people who are both feared and disliked and with whom relations are frequently hostile (e.g. the Dasyus, Dāsas and the Paṇis).

The Later Vedic literature – primarily the compositions associated with the *Sāma*, *Yajur*, and *Atharva Veda*s – depicts a recognizable change in material culture. The geographical focus includes the Punjab and the middle Ganga valley in the main, with a more marginal familiarity with the Indus area, western and eastern India and the Vindhyas. The society is essentially agrarian with little presence of urban centres. There is a considerable acquaintance with iron technology. Frequent mention is made of rice *(vrīhi)* which is not mentioned in the *Ṛgveda*. The clan identity continues and in many cases is extended to territorial identity. The Ṛgvedic deities do not have the pre-eminent position which they had had earlier since equal importance is now given to more recently incorporated deities. The fourfold *varṇa* structure mentioned only once in the late *Ṛgveda* is now a recognized feature. The geographical and philosophical connections with west Asia have weakened. There appears to be a greater assimilation with local cultures. In comparing the early and late Vedic texts the major characteristic of continuity remains the language, Vedic Sanskrit, but not without some change. This is also indicated by the writing of etymologies and grammars.

Whatever our cherished notions about the Aryans maybe, the archaeological evidence does not suggest a massive invasion or a single, massive migration.[14] Even if it be conceded that the presence of Indo-Aryan in the north-west can be attributed to invasion, as suggested by conflicts in the *Ṛgveda,* the same reason cannot be given for its presence in other parts of northern India. At most it can be said that the Indo-Aryan speakers were small groups of migrants with a strong adherence to a linguistic equipment initially deriving from Indo-European. The linguistic evidence points to the Indo-Aryan speakers living in the vicinity of those who spoke an alien language *(mṛdhra vāc)* and those later called the *mlecchas*.[15] Were these the Munda or Dravidian speakers? Were they also the authors of pre-iron Chalcolithic cultures? In the Ganga valley archaeological evidence does not suggest that the earlier inhabitants fled or migrated. Therefore their continued presence must have necessitated a process of acculturation. What then was the nature of the impact of these Indo-Aryan speakers? Perhaps it would make greater historical sense if we see it not as the imposition of Aryan culture on the existing Indian cultures, but rather, as the diffusion of Indo-Aryan. The new language could have been accepted for various reasons without necessitating the imposition of an entirely new culture.[16]

In the study of the interaction of cultures there are many facets which require investigation. Let me start with the most primary, the question of the numbers of people involved. This would imply demographic studies of various sites and settlements. Comparative assessments of population figures from the sites of varying cultures could be helpful, as also the detailed charting of the location of sites – whether they are superimposed or adjacent. Would there be a greater possibility of cross-cultural assimilation if the numbers are consistently small and equally matched?[17] A demographic analysis, even if impressionistic, studied together with the nature of the terrain and technology and facilities for transportation would provide indications of the pace and flow of migration. For instance, the Painted Grey Ware settlements being generally small, the nature of the terrain being thick jungle, the pace of migration would be slow even if the river was used as the main channel of communication. It should not be forgotten that in spite of a time-span of about six hundred years the geographical distribution of the Painted Grey Ware remains broadly the Ganga-Yamuna doāb and the Hakra valley. However, acceleration in the pace of communication seems to accompany the development of an urban culture as it would appear from the distribution of the Northern Black Polished Ware, in a comparable period.

Even a rough demographic picture will introduce an element of reality into the study. If the settlements of a particular culture are small then production is also likely to be small. A comparison between such data and literary descriptions of extravagant wealth may lead to a correcting of the poetic licence implicit in great works of literature. Estimates of production are relevant to the study of towns owing to the interdependence of towns and villages.[18] More mundane factors such as food habits have their own significance. The Ṛgvedic people had a diet substantially of barley and wheat, and the Later Vedic literature introduces rice. From the archaeological evidence we know that the Harappans were mainly barley and wheat eating, whereas the Ganga valley, the Banas valley and probably a part of western India was predominantly rice eating.[19] This points to a major difference of staple diet between the Ṛgvedic and Later Vedic people. If they were the same ethnically then they must have rapidly adjusted to a change of diet. However the Painted Grey Ware levels in the Doāb suggest a people long accustomed to rice. It is interesting that in later Sanskrit literature wheat is sometimes referred to as *mleccha bhojana*.[20]

Another aspect in the process of acculturation is the role of technology. A language which is associated with an advanced technology can often make a very effective impact. The use of the horse and of iron would point to an advanced technology. The acceptance of the Indo-Aryan language would therefore not require the physical conquest of the areas where it came to be spoken but rather the control of the advanced technology by the speakers of Indo-Aryan.[21] The horse-drawn chariot seems to have swung the balance militarily in favour of the Indo-Aryan speakers, judging from the hymns of the *Ṛgveda*. The horse as compared to the ox was a swifter means of transportation as also was the chariot as compared with the cart.[22] The introduction of iron did not mean entirely new technological implements. It was more a qualitative improvement of existing forms particularly in relation to the ecological conditions of the region. The hafted copper axe gave way to the socketed iron axe, the wooden plough had an iron tip added to it and the stone hoe was replaced by the iron hoe (or it was introduced where the hoe was not known before), not to mention adzes, arrow-heads, spear-heads, knives, daggers, nails, etc.[23] The technology of the Painted Grey Ware culture seems to support this assessment. The question of who first used iron technology in India has its own importance, but for our purposes it is more relevant to enquire as to whether the speakers of Indo-Aryan exploited the knowledge of iron technology to their advantage. That the new technology was essentially the improvement of existing forms is supported by the use of certain significant words in Vedic literature which appear to have a non-Indo-Aryan origin. Thus the most frequently used word for plough is *lāṅgala* which is of Munda origin and the word for rice *vrīhi* is believed to be of Dravidian origin.[24] Could there have been a correlation between the degree of technological change and the utilization of Indo-Aryan? That the caste status of iron smiths ultimately became low would accord with the probability that as long as the control of the technology lay with the higher status groups, the actual working of the technology could remain with low status groups.[25]

In ancient agricultural societies, apart from agricultural technology, another factor of some consequence would be the knowledge of the calendar. It is thought that the earliest calendar used in India was the lunar calendar. Yet the solar calendar was more efficient in its application to agriculture and astronomy (and thereby to astrology). The discovery and use of the solar calendar would require more advanced knowledge in mathematics and astronomy. A basis of mathematical knowledge must be assumed in order to explain the construction of the Harappan cities. Was this knowledge continued in some tradition? If the Harappans had used a binary system (by and large) then the decimal system referred to in the Vedic literature would have been an improvement.[26] The essential mathematical knowledge necessary for evolving a solar calendar may have been inherent in the requirements for the construction of complex sacrificial altars.[27] There appears to be a groping towards understanding the principles of the solar calendar in the Vedic literature. The year of 360 days (30 x 12 months) was known to be defective and attempts were made at intercalation in which the 366-day year was not excluded.[28] The widespread knowledge of the solar calendar is associated with Greek contacts at a later period. It is not to be ruled out however that a secret knowledge or a restricted knowledge of it may have existed earlier. The appropriation of such knowledge by certain groups may well have given them access to power and influence. A scientific study of the application of astronomy and mathematics to activities such as agriculture and astrology within the context of contemporary society might be revealing: as also the transmission of mathematical ideas between West Asia and India.

In the post-Harappa period the centre of historical activity moved away from the Indus valley towards other directions: to the Ganga valley with Magadha eventually emerging as a nuclear region, to western India, and later, to the coastal regions of the peninsula. Part of the reason for the movement away from the Indus valley was the breakdown in the Harappan economic system.[29] The sites in western India appear to have re-introduced the earlier maritime contacts with Mesopotamia, from at least the first millennium BC. As such, western India would have acted as a point of communication for goods and ideas between India and west Asia. A further archaeological investigation of the west coast and routes from here to the Ganga valley may prove worthwhile.[30]

Another aspect worth considering in assessing the reasons for the spread of Indo-Aryan is the interrelationship between language and society. The fact that the earliest Sanskrit grammars were written in the north points to a greater use or longer tradition of the language in this region. By contrast the lower Ganga valley retains a Prākṛt tradition for a longer period.[31] Was this distinction due to the linguistic differences in Indo-Aryan itself or was it due to a greater influence of non-Indo-Aryan languages in eastern India? Magadha is described as an impure land and the people of Aṅga, Vaṅga and Kaliṅga are referred to as *mleccha*.[32] It is also worth examining why certain important words relating to technology were introduced from non-Indo-Aryan sources and retained in Indo-Aryan. We have already noticed the case of *lāṅgala* and *vrīhi*. The Indo-Aryan for horse is *aśva,* yet *aśva* was never as commonly used in the Late Indo-Aryan languages as *ghoṭa* and its derivatives. That this could happen with items as important as the plough, rice and the horse, makes one wonder whether the question of loan words from Munda and Dravidian does not call for a co-ordinated study by the specialist in linguistics and the historian, which would not merely trace the loan or the etymology of words, but would also throw light on the cultural context of their incorporation. The etymology of technical and professional words in their historical context would alone be worth a study.[33]

It is historically well-known that in the spread of a language associated with an advanced technology it is often the dominant groups in the existing society which take up the new language first. This would be easier to understand in our period if we had some concrete evidence on the origin of the caste structure. It is curious that although the origin of the caste structure is frequently associated with the Aryan speakers it occurs only in India and not in other societies which were also recipients of Aryan culture. It may therefore have been a pre-Aryan system which was reconstituted somewhat, and described in Later Vedic literature. To see caste as the distinction between fair Aryans and dark-non-Aryans is to mock at a very complex system. In the study of social structure the historian of ancient India must of necessity now take the help of social anthropology. The essentials of a caste society are, firstly, marriage and lineage functioning through exogamous and endogamous kinship relations *(jāti);* secondly, the integration of the division of labour into a hierarchical system which eventually takes the form of service relationships; thirdly, the idea of pollution where some groups are seen as ritually pure, others less so and yet others totally impure or polluting; and finally the association of castes with particular geographical locations. All these factors could have been present in the Harappa culture where social stratification can at least be surmised.[34] If a similar system prevailed in the Banas culture and those of the Ganga valley, then the spread of a new language could be achieved through influencing the groups which held high status and by rearrangement of endogamous groups.[35]

Ascribing caste status did not merely depend on the occupation of a group. In some cases an entire tribe was ascribed a particular rank. Those speaking a non-Indo-Aryan language were frequently given a low rank and described as *mleccha*. In the case of the *cāṇḍāla*s there is reference to a *cāṇḍāla-bhāṣā*. [36] Some of these tribes remained consistently of low status over many centuries, such as the Kirāta and the Pulinda;[37] others acquired political power and thereby higher status. Even today there are pockets of Munda and Dravidian speaking people in areas of Indo-Aryan languages. This is not due to any historical oversight. The Munda-speaking groups until recently were hunters and pastoralists with, at most, digging-stick agriculture. In contrast to this the Indo-Aryan speaking people are, by and large, plough-and hoe-using agriculturalists. Did the Aryanization of language accompany the expansion of the iron-using agrarian village?

This village was not the neolithic village growing essentially in isolation, nor the chalcolithic village with restricted trade inter-relationships. It was the more prosperous iron-using village whose prosperity increased with easier access to both iron ore and more land for cultivation. This could not only give these villages a political edge over the others but also provide a larger surplus for those in control. At one level this became the stable base for the growth of towns;[38] at another level it strengthened the language, Indo-Aryan.

With the expansion of agro-pastoralism to include settled agrarian villages, tribal identity was extended to territorial identity, as is reflected in tribal and clan names being given to geographical areas. These developments led to the emergence of caste and private property.[39] The state with both monarchical and non-monarchical forms of government evolved from these changes.

Even among clans that had accepted the new technology and language, the priests – those that claimed to be the ritually pure groups – would have resisted the new culture unless their own status was safeguarded. Was this done by allowing them to preserve their ritual purity through the caste structure and by their continuing to hold a priestly status, and also by incorporating much of their religion into the new culture? The assimilation of a tribe into the caste structure would also require some assimilation of its religion. The religious aspects of Later Vedic literature, inasmuch as they differ from the *Ṛgveda,* include a large amount of non-Aryan practice and belief – both at the level of ritual and of deities.[40] It is indeed a moot point whether this religious literature evolved from a single culture.

Every society has a method of remembering what it regards as the important aspects of its past and this is woven into its historical tradition: for the pre-medieval period the *itihāsa-purāṇa* traditions set out to record the past. A significant section of these traditions is the preservation of the genealogies and myths associated with rulers. The succession genealogies (*vaṃśāvalī*) may not always be historically correct but they can be seen as an attempt to map the pattern of the migration and spread of various peoples.

Such an analysis can be more useful than the repeated but so far unsuccessful attempts to identify the tribes as either Aryan or non-Aryan. Genealogies have played a noticeably important part in the Indian historical tradition, even when they are known to be fabricated. This is surely the clue to understanding the role of the genealogy, not necessarily as an authentic chronicle but rather as a social document. Similarly, what is important about the myths is not whether they are historically authentic, but the cultural assumptions of the society which are implicit in the myth.[41]

The questions which arise in the study of the proto-historic period have a relevance to later history. It would seem that in northern India the expansion of the village economy based on iron technology accompanied the diffusion of Indo-Aryan, judging by the archaeological evidence for the distribution of iron in association with literary evidence for Indo-Aryan. Indo-Aryan therefore would not be widely accepted in those areas where iron technology was already known. In the peninsula the area covered by the iron-using Megalithic sites roughly coincides with the area of the widespread use of Dravidian languages.

If we can explain the reasons for the shift in focus from the Indus valley to the Ganga valley in proto-historic times, then we can also throw some light on one of the more interesting facets of ancient Indian history, namely, the geographical shift in the nuclear regions which were the matrices of large states and empires. At least three regions come immediately to mind: Magadha, the Raichur-Bijapur districts, and the area between Kanchipuram and Tanjore. Why did these regions give rise to a series of politically dominant states and then go into quiescence?[42] Was it due to the fertility of the region yielding large revenues, or the abundant availability of iron, or access to trade routes, or the exploitation of a new technology, or the rise of ideologies motivating political action? Or was it merely the strange but happy coincidence of a series of strong rulers, which is the explanation generally offered?

In the analysis of social structure there is a need for redefining social relationships. To see caste only in terms of the four-fold *varṇa* does not take us very far. One would like to know how tribes and social groups were adjusted into the caste hierarchy and assigned a caste status. The theory that the caste-structure was initially flexible but gradually became rigid and allowed of little mobility, is now open to question. There is enough evidence to suggest that there have been in all periods deviations from the theoretical concept of caste.[43] We also know that there was a continual emergence of new castes for a variety of reasons. Furthermore social change presupposes social tension and at times even conflicts between groups, and these are referred to in the sources. The origin, nature and consequences of these tensions constitutes another significant area of study.

The history of religion, apart from its theological, philosophical and iconographical aspects, also has a social aspect, since religion has to be practised by people in order to be viable. The interrelation therefore of religious cults and movements with social groups is very close. What were the social roots of Buddhism and Jainism? Why were certain cults assimilated and others left out in what later came to be called Hinduism? What accounts for the remarkable popularity of the mother-goddess cults in various forms particularly in the post-Gupta period? More precise answers to such questions would help us ascertain with greater accuracy the nature of the 'brahmanical renaissance' as it has been called in the Gupta and post-Gupta periods.

It will be evident that I am making a plea for more intensive studies of the nature of society in ancient India: and by this I mean an integrated understanding of the many facets which go into the functioning of a society. Such a study involves not merely additional dimensions in terms of methods and sources, it also means, if need be, altering the perspective from which we view the past. New perspectives, although they may initially appear whimsical, often provide new insights. The immense labour and scholarship of our predecessors has provided us with a firm foundation on which to base our studies of ancient Indian history. We can with confidence, therefore, explore new perspectives. Ultimately as historians we are concerned not merely with attempting to discover the past, but with trying to understand it.

Notes and References

1. T. R. Trautmann, *The Aryans and British India,* Delhi, 1997.
2. The Aryan problem arose out of a series of philological studies in the eighteenth and nineteenth century which recorded the similarities between a number of languages of Asia and Europe and postulated a common ancestry in Indo-European (T. R. Trautmann, *The Aryans and British India,* Delhi, 1997). Max Müller's statement about the Aryan nation as the physical manifestation of Aryan culture lent support to the search for the Aryan race. His later repeated attempts to deny the existence of an Aryan race were often ignored *(Biographies of Words and the Home of the Vedas,* 1887, p. 90). Incidentally, it is conceivable that Max Müller's Aryan-Semitic dichotomy may well have influenced the Aryan-Dravidian dichotomy. The real damage was caused by his assertion of the superiority of Aryan culture over all other cultures, which has been made axiomatic to the study of the Indian past *(Chips from a German Workshop,* 1867, I, p. 63. ' ... In continual struggle with each other and with Semitic and Turanian races, these Aryan nations have become the rulers of history, and it seems to be their mission to link all parts of the world together by chains of civilisation, commerce and religion ...'.) Aryan culture is often taken as the starting point of Indian culture and is projected both backwards (in attempts to prove the Aryan basis of the Harappa culture) and forwards in time. It is also sought to be associated with every worthwhile achievement in early India.

   In his enthusiasm for the Aryan way of life (as he saw it), Max Müller further depicted Aryan society as an idyllic society of village communities where people were concerned not with the mundane things of everyday living but with other-worldly thoughts and values (*India, What Can It Teach Us?* pp. 101ff.). This has also acted as a check on the more realistic study of the actual conditions of life in the Vedic period. That the motives of Max Müller and other Indologists of his view in acclaiming Aryan culture derived from a genuine admiration for Aryan society as they saw it, may up to a point be conceded, but this does not exonerate them from gilding the lily. Max Müller's attempt to link India and Europe via the Aryans was in part to connect the origins of Indian culture with the founders of European culture. Thus Indian culture could acquire status in the eyes of Europe and, at the same time, early Indian nationalism could exploit this connection to combat the cultural inferiority complex generated among Indians as a result of British rule. In fact early Indian nationalism gave greater attention to extolling the Aryans in India rather than to the connection with Europe. Historical scholarship has now moved beyond the needs and confines of nineteenth century nationalism and a re-evaluation of Max Müller's theories is necessary.

Even some modern sociological theorists have made sweeping generalisations on contemporary India and Indian society on the basis of the nineteenth century understanding of Indian history. Max Weber in his study, *The Religion of India* (New York 1967 reprint) used fairly uncritically much of the writing of Orientalists such as Max Müller. A more recent example of the acceptance of this tradition, without a sufficient investigation of the alternatives, is Louis Dumont's *Homo Hierarchicus* (1967). That the influence of such thinking, stressing the other-worldly character of Indian society, is apparent even on economic historians is evident from Gunnar Myrdal, *Asian Drama* (1969), where the Weberian thesis is given considerable emphasis to explain the failure of the development of capitalism in India.

3. Asko Parpola et al., *Decipherment of the Proto-Dravidian Inscriptions of the Indus Civilisation,* The Scandinavian Institute of Asian Studies, Copenhagen, 1969; Asko Parpola, *Progress in the Decipherment of the Proto-Dravidian Indus Script,* 1969; Asko Parpola, *Further Progress in the Decipherment of the Proto-Indus Script*, 1969.

A less publicised attempt was made by a number of Russian scholars. Y. Knorozov, *Proto-Indica,* 1968.

Owing to a lack of a bi-lingual inscription most attempts so far have used a system of intelligent (and in some cases not so intelligent) guesswork. Using the inconographic representation as the starting point attempts have been made to try and read the script as that of an Indo-Aryan language (Wadell, S. K. Ray, Krishna Rao, S. R. Rao). Those who have used the script as their starting point have more often arrived at Proto-Dravidian (Hunter, Heras, the Russians and the Finns). The Finns read it as a largely logographic script based on the principles of homophony. The advance made by the Finnish scholars and to some extent the earlier Russian studies is that they have placed greater reliance on linguistic and mathematical techniques rather than on historical guesswork. Any claims to decipherment must satisfy certain preconditions. The decipherment must conform to a grammatical and linguistic system and cannot be arbitrary (this being the major objection to the attempt by Krishna Rao and S. R. Rao); it must conform to the archaeological evidence of the culture and to the chronological span of the Harappa culture; the reading of the inscriptions must make sense in terms of the context of the culture. Of the recent attempts, the Russian and the Finnish conform most to these preconditions. However even their readings present problems which they have not satisfactorily overcome. [A. Parpola, *Deciphering the Indus Script*, Cambridge 1994].

4. As for example in the essays of Sylvain Levi, Jean Przyluski and Jules Bloch, translated and published by P. C. Bagchi in *Pre-Aryan and Pre-Dravidian in India,* 1929, and in the writings of S. K. Chatterjee, T. Burrow and M. B. Emeneau. [F. C. Southworth, *Linguistic Archaeology of South Asia*, London 2005; M. M. Deshpande and P. Hook (eds.), *The Indo-Aryans of Ancient South Asia*, Berlin 1995].

5. A. Ghosh, 'The Indus Civilisation – Its Origins, Authors, Extent and Chronology', in V. N. Misra and N.S. Mate (eds), *Indian Pre-history,* 1964. An attempt has been made to try and identify the Sothi Culture with the Ṛgvedic people by A. D. Pusalkar, 'Pre-Harappan, Harappan and Post-Harappan Culture and the Aryan Problem', *The Quarterly Review of Historical Studies,* VII, no. 4, 1967-68, pp. 233ff. Apart from the problem that the geographical extent does not coincide, since the Ṛgvedic culture included northern Punjab and excluded Sind and western India, there is also the problem of chronology. Attempts to date the *Ṛgveda* to the fourth and fifth millennia BC are based mainly on references to astronomical positions mentioned in the texts, viz., Tilak, *The Orion* ... ; Jacobi, 'On the Date of the *Ṛgveda'*, *Indian Antiquary,* June 1894; and Bühler, *Indian Antiquary,* Sept. 1894. Such evidence is not conclusive, since references to astronomy could have been incorporated from the traditions of an earlier people. The parallels with Gāthic Avestan and with Kassite and Hittite inscriptions which are very close, would date the *Ṛgveda* to the middle of the second millennium BC.

6. The attempted identification of the Harappa culture with the later Vedic society on the basis of both being agro-urban societies is again controverted by the differences not only in the total culture but also in the geographical nuclei [G. L. Possehl (ed.), *The Harappan Civilization*, New Delhi 1982; M. R. Mughal, *Ancient Cholistan*, Lahore 1997]. The Harappa culture is located in the Indus valley and western India and its urbanization is based on a chalcolithic system with an absence of iron. Later Vedic society centering on the Ganga valley from which the Harappa culture is largely absent (except for a few sites in the Doāb) owes its gradual urbanization in part to iron technology. The technology of the two cultures is different. The pre-eminent role of the fertility cult among the Harappans is absent in Vedic society. The Harappans buried their dead, the Vedic people largely cremated their dead. (It is interesting that so far no graves have been found in association with the Painted Grey Ware cultures, which may suggest that they cremated their dead). The horse so characteristic of Vedic society is not associated with the Mature Harappans. The Harappa culture from the very beginning used a script whereas references to writing in Vedic society come at a later stage. If, finally, the Harappan script is read as Proto-Dravidian then there will be hardly any possibility of identifying the Harappa culture with Indo-Aryan speakers.

7. A. H. Dani, 'Gandhara Grave Culture', *Ancient Pakistan,* III, 1967.

8. B. B. Lal, *Indian Archaeology—*A *Review,* 1959-60 (for the site of Gilund); D. P. Agarwal, 'C-14 Dates, Banas Culture and the Aryans', *Current Science,* 5 March 1966, pp. 114ff.; H. D. Sankalia, 'New Light on the Indo-Iranian or Western Asiatic Relations between 1700–1200 BC', *Artibus Asiae,* XXVI, 1963; H. D. Sankalia, S.B. Deo, Z. D. Ansari, *Excavations at Ahar,* 1969 [D. Chakrabarti, *Indian Archaeology*, Delhi 2006].

9. B. B. Lal, 'Further Copper Hoards from the Gangetic Basin and a Review of the Problem', *Ancient India,* no. 7, 1951, pp. 20ff; S. P. Gupta, 'Indian Copper Hoards', *Journal of the Bihar Research Society,* 49, 1963, pp. 147ff.

10. B. B. Lal, 'Excavations at Hastinapur', *Ancient India,* nos. 10 and 11, 1954-55, pp. 5ff; T.N. Roy, 'Stratigraphical Position of the Painted Grey Ware in the Gangetic Valley', *Bharati,* no. 8, II, 1964-65, pp. 64ff.

11. A summary of attempts to identify the Aryans with archaeological evidence is that of Dilip K. Chakrabarti, 'The Aryan Hypothesis in Indian Archaeology', *Indian Studies,* IX, no. 4, July–Sept. 1968, pp. 343ff. The evidence of the Gandhara Grave Culture has been interpreted by Dani as representing perhaps, the early Indo-Aryan migration identified with the Ṛgvedic literature. The linguistic theories of Hoernle and Grierson, suggesting that there were two bands of migration and therefore of language, have been used in the argument that the first band settled in the Punjab, and the second, skirting round the Indus, perhaps settled in the Banas valley. From here there was a movement both along the northern slopes of the Vindhyas to Bihar and also into the Doāb. Incidentally, in the latter case it would have followed a route which was frequently used in historical times to connect the Doāb with the west coast.

12. There are incidental references to migration in the *Ṛgveda,* in verses such as 1.30.9; 1.36.18; and they read clearly as for example, VI.45.1, '*... ya ānayat parāvataḥ sūnītī turvaśam yaduṁ indraḥ sa no yuvā sakhā ...*'. Furthermore it must be remembered that the *nadī stuti* hymn which is often quoted to contradict the theory of migration is in fact from the tenth *maṇḍala* of the *Ṛgveda* which is late and composed after the settlements in the Doāb.

13. The element of doubt arises because of the meaning of theword *ayas*. It is possible that it originally meant copper, as it seems to in some contexts, but later with the introduction of iron it was qualified by the terms *kṛṣṇa ayas* and *śyāma ayas*. When the association of *tāmra* with copper became common, then *ayas* may have been reserved for iron. It has however been argued that *ayas* originally meant iron and that the earliest knowledge of iron in India has therefore to be associated with the Ṛgvedic people. L. Gopal, *Uttar Bharati,* IV, no. 3, pp. 71ff and N. R. Banerjee, *The Iron Age in India,* pp. 158ff. The Indo-European root of *ayas* and its consistent use as iron in other Indo-European languages *aes, ais, aisa, eisarn* is a strong argument in favour of this view. This could date the *Ṛgveda* to c. 1000 BC, consistent with the archaeological date for iron in the nort-west.

14. The migration theory would seem more acceptable than the invasion theory. The association of the Cemetry H evidence with the Aryans and the supposed massacre at Mohenjo-daro has been doubted. B. B. Lal, 'Protohistoric Investigations', *Ancient India,* no. 9, 1953, p. 88; G. F. Dales, 'The Mythical Massacre at Mohenjo-daro', *Expedition,* VI, no. 3, 1964, pp. 36ff; A. Ghosh, 'The Archaeological Back-

ground', *M.A.S.I.*, no. 9, 1962, p. 1; G. F. Dales, 'The Decline of the Harappans', *Scientific American,* vol. 214, no. 5, 1966. There is no evidence of Kalibangan having been attacked and it is unlikely that it would have been spared, being so close, if Harappa had been attacked. Post-Harappan cultures rarely build directly on the debris of Harappan sites except at Rupar and Alamgirpur. The extremely interesting discussion by Burrow on the significance of the terms *arma* and *armaka* in the Vedic literature and Pāṇini *(Journal of Indian History,* XLI, 1963, part 1, pp. 159ff) suggests that the references to ruins were to the Indus Civilization cities. What is curious however is that in some cases it would appear that Indra and Agni were responsible for the destruction of these cities, whereas in other cases they appear already to have been in ruins. It would seem that most of these cities were in the Sarasvatī and Punjab region. It is stated that the dark inhabitants fled and migrated. This would agree with the archaeological evidence that the cities were deserted and not occupied by the new arrivals. They were regarded as places of evil and the haunt of sorceresses *(yātumatī)* and therefore to be avoided. This would hardly be the attitude of a conquering people who had actually destroyed the cities. Could the cities have been deserted, owing to a natural calamity before the arrival of the Indo-Aryan speakers, who associated the ruins of cities with evil, perhaps set fire to the remaining ruins and ultimately attributed the destruction of the cities to Indra and Agni? This would also explain the chronological gap, i.e., the Harappa culture having declined by 1750 BC and the Ṛgvedic Aryans being dated to *circa* 1500 BC.

Skeleton analysis of the Harappa culture sites tend to puncture the theory of the Indo-Aryan speakers representing a large and separate racial group. S. S. Sarkar, *Ancient Races of Baluchistan, Punjab and Sind,* maintains that the Harappans were the same as the present-day predominant ethnic types living in these areas, which would contradict the theory of a large scale Aryan invasion or migration. But since the present day population of these areas has been heavily infiltrated by people from Afghanistan and the borderlands in the course of historical incursions, this analysis suggests that the Harappans in this area were also infiltrators from the borderlands who mixed with local populations. Dr K. Sen, 'Ancient Races of India and Pakistan, a Study of Methods', *Ancient India,* nos. 20 and 21, 1964-65, pp. 178ff, has suggested that the ethnic stock of Cemetry R37 and Cemetry H appears to have been the same although there are cultural differences.

15. In describing the *dāsa* the references to their being overcome in raids are fewer than the large number of other references to the differences between *ārya* and *dāsa*. These differences emphasise the fact of the latter having an alien culture. Thus the *dāsa* are described in the *Ṛgveda* as *hatvī dasyūn pura āyasīrni tārit* (II, 20.8)*; yo dāsam varṇam* (II.12.4); *hatvī dasyūn prāryan varṇam āvat* (III, 34.9); *ayajvānaḥ* (I.33.4); *māyāvān abrahmā dasyurartā* (IV.16. 9); *anāsa* (V.29.10); *akarmā dasyūr abhi no amantur anyavrato amanuṣaḥ tvam tasyāmitrahan vadhar dāsasya dambhaya* (X.22.8); *mṛdhra vāc* (V.29.10), etc.

    The word *mleccha* occurs, for example, in the *Śatapatha Brāhmaṇa,* III.2.1.23-24, and is essentially a term of contempt for those who cannot speak the Aryan language and only gradually comes to acquire the meaning of a barbarian in a cultural sense. The etymology of the word is uncertain and does not appear to be Indo-Aryan, although it is said to derive from *vāc*. It is also said to be onomatopoeic, based on the strange sounds of an alien tongue. A reference to *milakhuka* (from Pali *milakkhu,* Sanskrit *mleccha*) in the *Vinaya Piṭaka,* III.28 is explained by Buddhaghoṣa as *Andha Damil ādi*. [R. Thapar, 'A Possible Identification of Meluhha, Dilmun and Makan', *JESHO,* 18, 1978, 1, 1–42].

16. It is not surprising that elsewhere too where Indo-European speakers have migrated and settled, the evidence for their presence is largely the Indo-European base of some of the languages of those areas. Greek contains elements of pre-Greek languages and the culture of classical Greece is rooted more in the pre-existing cultures of the region than in Indo-European culture (Luigi Pareti, *The Ancient World,* part I; Moses Finlay, *The Ancient Greeks;* George Thompson, *Studies in Ancient Greek Society).* The culture of the Hittites is derived from the Hattians and only the language is Indo-European. The Mitannis worshipped 'Aryan' gods and used technical terms for chariotry which are Indo-European, but their language Hurrian is not included in the Indo-European group. Similarly some Kassites had Aryan-sounding names but only their ruling class seems to have been familiar with the Indo-European language. The idea of a common culture of the Indo-European speakers grew out of philological evidence. Archaeological evidence does not support such an idea. It might be worthwhile for philologists to reconsider the question of how common in fact was the culture of the Indo-European speakers. Clearly there was an early stage when certain ideas and perhaps some

institutions were common. This stage is reflected in, for example, parts of the *Ṛgveda,* the Avestan *Gāthās,* the inscriptions of the Hittites and passages of Homer. This forms the starting point of the ideas on comparative mythology developed for instance in the Kuhn-Müller theory and in the writings of George Dumezil and Paul Thieme, which theories were applied to other areas on the basis of philological evidence. Had the spread of the language also resulted in the spread of similar ideas and institutions then there would have been a far greater identity in the subsequent development of the cultures of the regions where Indo-European languages were spoken. S. C. Malik in *Indian Civilisation, The Formative Period* (1969), p. 144, refers to the Aryan superstructure of ideology being imposed upon the earlier socio-economic organization. 'Hence, it was contrary to the general opinion, not the Aryanisation of India, but rather the Indianisation of the Aryan nomadic pastoralist hordes.'

17. The large concentration of people in the Harappan towns immediately indicates a different type of organization from the smaller settlements of other Chalcolithic cultures. Even when describing the Harappan cities it is sobering to remember that Kalibangan for instance could hardly have had a population larger than 5,000. In cases where a series of trenches have been cut across a mound it is possible to assess the increase or decrease of population in an area of habitation at particular periods by comparing the stratigraphy. For example, a comparative study on these lines of PG Ware levels and NBP levels could provide considerable information for particular sites. Population estimates are, of course, best carried out from the evidence of burials and of habitation sites uncovered in a horizontal excavation. Where the latter is not possible, a controlled series of soundings may help. Palaeo-demography has already attracted the attention of scholars after the pioneering work of Matiga half a century ago. Attempts have been made to compute population by studying the relative density of remains, by estimating the mean number of individuals in a village site through the habitations and the burials, the land-man ratio in the context of the technology of the period, the estimated number of persons required for a co-operative effort, the setting-up of menhirs, and by a variety of statistical methods.

18. Attempts can be made to estimate the nature of food production by calculating the area of land required to feed a given number of people on the basis of the agricultural technology, crops and possible soil conditions of the time. The inter-relation of town and village raises

the question of the precise use of the term 'urban'. Does it refer to a fortified village, or a town or a city? The Indo-European root of *pur* means a sorrounding wall, therefore although in later periods the word *pura* referred to a town, in the early period it could have been just a walled settlement [W. Rau, *The Meaning of Pur in Vedic Literature*, Munich 1976]. A distinction has also to be maintained between the village which becomes an important market and thus the focus of the region, and the town. These distinctions in the degrees of urbanization are relevant not only to the study of prehistory but also in historical periods.

19. The words *dhānya* meaning grain, and *yava* barley or grain, occur in the *Ṛgveda* and in Later Vedic literature. Specific words for rice, of which the most frequent is *vrīhi* and others are *taṇḍula* and *śāli* occur in the *Atharvaveda,* VI.140.2, etc.; S. K. Chatterjee suggests a possible Dravidian origin for *vrīhi* in *arichi* (History and Culture of the Indian People, vol. I, *The Vedic Age,* p. 1449). Wheat is referred to as *godhuma* in Later Vedic literature. It is still not certain whether the rice remains at Lothal indicate rice cultivation or merely a wild variety growing in the marshes (Visnu Mittre, unpublished paper read at Patna in 1969, 'Environmental Backgróund to the Neolithic-Chalcolithic Complex in North-Western India'). Archaeological evidence suggests that rice was the staple food in a major part of the subcontinent during this period. The use of the word *dhānya* for paddy is late.

20. As for example in the *Trikāṇḍaśeṣa,* a supplement to the *Nāmaliṅgānuśāsana* of Amarsiṁha, by Puruṣottamadeva, who is said to have flourished in the court of Lakṣmaṇasena in the twelfth century AD.

21. It is not entirely coincidental that the spread of Indo-European elsewhere is frequently associated with the arrival of the horse-drawn chariot and on occasion with iron technology.

22. It is curious that there should be no substantial remains of at least the metal parts of the chariot in various excavations; and particularly at Harappa and Mohenjo-daro if we are to accept the theory that these cities were invaded by the Ṛgvedic people or that there was an extensive use of the chariot and the spoked wheel in these cities [See also, P. Raulwing, *Horses, Chariots and Indo-Europeans*, Budapest 2000]. This is in striking contrast to the evidence from Egypt where the new arrivals in their horse-drawn chariots are depicted clearly in

reliefs and engravings on stone. The chariot of the Vedic texts was light, had spoked wheels, could accommodate three persons and was horse-drawn. It was therefore speedier, had greater manoeuvrability and consequently the two combatants had a vantage position (O. R. Gurney, *The Hittites,* pp. 104ff and S. Piggott, *Prehistoric India,* pp. 273ff).

23. The significance of these improvements is that the socketed iron axe is more efficient in a heavily forested region, the iron hoe makes a substantial difference in rice cultivation where more continual weeding is necessary than in other crops. This is also suggested in one of the frequently used words for 'hoe' in Vedic literature, *stambhaghna,* literally that which destroys clumps. The importance of the iron hoe has not received sufficient attention in the evaluation of technological change during this period.

24. The Munda derivation of *lāṅgala* is discussed by J. Przyluski in Bagchi (ed.), *Pre-Aryan and Pre-Dravidian in India,* pp. 8ff;also in T. Burrow, *The Sanskrit Language,* p. 379. It occurs as *nāngal* in Dravidian (Dravidian Etymological Dictionary, No. 2368). All attempt to associate it with the Indo-European *leg/leng* as in J. Pokorny, *Vergleichens des Worterbuch der Indo-Germanischen Sprachen* and thereby to link it with *Nirukta,* VI.26 of Yāska has not been accepted for linguistic reasons (S. K. Chatterjee, 'Non-Aryan Elements in Indo-Aryan', *JGIS,* III.42). It could be added that even from the point of view of the technology of the plough, the ploughshare is the central object and not an attachment.

The early occurrence of the word for 'plough' in non-Indo-Aryan languages would invalidate the suggestion that the Aryan speakers introduced the plough. The possibility that the plough may have been known to the Harappans on the basis of a particular sign in the script resembling the Sumerian sign for plough has now been confirmed by excavations at Kalibangan which uncovered the furrow marks in a field outside the city's fortification which date to the pre-Harappan period. On a purely impressionistic view it seems unlikely that a sufficient food surplus could have been produced to maintain the cities without plough agriculture.

25. In the *Saṁhitā* literature the *karmāra* is respected, but gradually his status becomes low. *Ṛgveda,* X.72.2; IX.112.2, *Atharvaveda,* III.5.6. Ultimately the *karmāra* is ranked with the *Niṣāda* and the *kulāla*. *Manu,* IV.215; Kane, *History of the Dharmashastras,* II, p.

73. The lowering of the status may have had to do with the fact that the smiths were possibly non-tribal artisans, (it has been suggested that the copper-smiths were itinerant smiths) who would be allowed commensality and participation in the ritual, but not marriage relationships with the tribe. The social rights and obligations of such professional groups would be worth examining.

26. The Harappan system of weights has been described as binary in the lower weights – 1, 2, 8/3, 16, 32, 64 ... and decimal in the higher weights. The decimal basis of counting is referred to in the *Taittirīya Saṁhitā,* IV.40.11.4; *Maitrāyaṇi Saṁhitā,* II.8.14; *Kāṭhaka Saṁhitā,* XVII.10 and XXXIX.6; *Vājasaneyi Saṁhitā,* XVII.2. There are references to ten raised to the power of twelve. The existence of the earlier binary system suggests that calculations may have been on the basis of the square. The commonly used cosmology of the Babylonians and Sumerians is believed to have had the mathematical base of the square. The use of both the square and circular cosmology in Indian sources at this time does suggest that new ideas on astronomy may have been in the air. There is a great likelihood that the circular theory was first developed among navigators, perhaps the Phoenicians, and would have then travelled to those in contact with the Phoenicians. C. P. S. Menon, *Early Astronomy and Cosmology,* pp. 36ff, makes an interesting correlation between the prevalence of the square cosmology and the circular cosmology in early India.

27. The need for exact geometrical knowledge arose in part because, although there were a variety of shapes permitted for altars such as the falcon, the chariot-wheel, the tortoise, the triangle, etc., their area had to be identical. The number of bricks was also prescribed. The geometrical principles involved in both creating precisely measured forms and converting one form into another are described in detail in the *Śulva Sūtras*. Admittedly most of these texts belong to the end of the Vedic period or even to the immediately post-Vedic period. Nevertheless they contain the developed and classified knowledge of geometry which must certainly have had earlier beginnings. This geometrical knowledge would be of use in other spheres of life as well, as for example in measuring land.

28. One year of twelve months comprising 360 days is frequently referred to in the *Ṛgveda,* 1.164.11; 1.164.48. A year of 366 days has been suggested on the basis of the Ribhus in *Ṛgveda,* IV.33.7. An intercalary month in a five-year circle finds mention in a late section

of the *Ṛgveda,* X.85.13. An intercalary thirteenth month of 30 days in a five-year circle occurs in the *Atharvaveda,* IX.9.19.

A primaeval element in Vedic society is indicated by the fact that magic is a substantial feature in both religious and technological concepts. It would be expected therefore that mathematical and astronomical knowledge would tend to be hidden in a mesh of symbolism and magic. That this element persists is apparent from the consultations with the village pandit which are still a part of the rural scene for determining the 'right day' for important agricultural activities such as sowing and harvesting. This has implications relating to the calendar as well as the notion of the auspicious day. The latter almost certainly derives its sanctity from the former.

29. In the Indus valley this would be caused by any or all of the following factors: the geological uplift at Sehwan resulting in the excessive flooding of the Indus near Mohenjo-daro or a change in the course of the Indus and the Sutlej; the salination of the soil; deforestation causing soil erosion and decrease in natural irrigation and thereby rendering agriculture difficult; and the termination specifically of the Harappan trade with Sumer encouraging de-urbanisation. Some of these factors are discussed by R. L. Raikes, 'The End of the Ancient Cities of the Indus', *American Anthropology,* 1964 and 'The Mohenjo-daro Floods', *Antiquity,* 40; G. F. Dales, 'New Investigations at Mohenjo-daro', *Archaeology,* 18, 1965; H. T. Lambrick, 'The Indus Flood Plain and the Indus Civilisation', *Geographical Journal,* 133, 1967. Detailed discussion of the Sumerian trade is available in L. Oppenheim, *Ancient Mesopotamia* and W. F. Leemans, *Foreign Trade in the Old Babylonian Period.* The breakdown in trade is supported by the fact that the dockyard at Lothal had fallen into disuse by *circa* 1800 BC (*Ancient India,* nos. 18 and 19, 1962-63, p. 213). [S. Ratnagar, *The End of the Great Harappan Tradition*, Delhi 2000].

30. The trade with Ophira during the reign of Solomon, the obelisk of Shalmanesar III depicting Indian elephants, the evidence of Indian teak at Mugheir and in the palace of Nebuchadnezzar and a variety of linguistic evidence (some of which is discussed in H. G. Rawlinson, *Intercourse between India and the Western World*, Cambridge 1916) would attest to trading contacts between India and the Near East. The *brāhmī* script may have originated in north-western India as a kind of merchant's code partially associated with the Semitic script, and in course of time and use in commerce, have travelled to the

Ganga valley. The *aramaic* adaptations in *kharoṣṭhī* clearly arose from commercial and administrative needs.

31. In the *Śatapatha Brāhmaṇa,* III.2.3.15 and the *Kauṣītaki Brāhmaṇa,* VII.6, the speech of the Kuru Pañcālas and the north generally is extolled and made a model for study. This ties in with the fact that Pāṇini is associated with the north. Yet the Punjab had been relegated to the status of a *mleccha deśa* in the *Atharvaveda,* V.22.14.

    The linguistic differences between the Punjab and the middle Ganga valley were earlier sought to be explained on the basis of the theory that there were two bands of Aryan speakers and this theory was developed by Hoernle, *A Grammar of the Eastern Hindi Compared with the Other Gaudian Languages,* 1880, and by G. Grierson, *Languages,* I.G.I., vol. I, 1907. S. K. Chatterjee and S. M. Katre in *Languages,* G.I. 1965, have preferred the argument that the differences are due to many more groups mutually interacting. What is perhaps called for at this stage is a comparative study of the linguistic structure of the various Prākrits and the pre-Aryan languages.

32. *Atharvaveda,* V.22.14; *Gopatha Brāhamaṇa,* II.9; *Vājasaneyi Saṁhitā,* XXX.5.22; *Taittirīya Brāhmaṇa,* III.4.1.1; *Baudhāyana Dharma Sūtra,* I.1.14.

33. Jules Bloch, 'Sanskrit and Dravidian', in Bagchi (ed.), *Pre-Aryan and Pre-Dravidian in India,* pp. 46ff. The use of the word *ghoṭa* in Sanskrit is late occurring in such texts as the *Āpastamba Śrauta Sūtra,* XV.3.12; *ghoṭaka* in *Pañcatantra,* V.10.4; *Vikramādityacarita,* etc. An early use of *ghoṭaka* in Pāli occurs in *Jātaka,* VI.452.

    A micro-study of the etymology of place-names, even contemporary place-names, would be revealing particularly in the context of early Munda and Dravidian settlement in northern India. Names such as Gaṅgā, Kaliṅga, Aṅga, Vaṅga, etc., have already been discussed as probable Munda names. Bagchi, *Pre-Aryan and Pre-Dravidian in India,* pp.72ff.

34. The pattern of settlement at Harappa, Mohenjo-daro, Kalibangan suggests an elite in residence on the citadel mound; the large and separate residential area to the east of the citadel occupied by lesser status groups; and the single or double-roomed 'workmen's quarters' indicating a third level of stratification. The question has often been asked as to who was in authority in the Harappa culture and how was authority maintained? The answer could lie in the existence of a

kind of caste structure, where a small group preserving itself through strict endogamous marriage and organizing its authority through a hierarchy of service relationships in which it was assigned a high status, and stressing its ritual purity, could have held power. The great Bath at Mohenjo-daro is now almost universally recognized as being indicative of an ablution ritual which could have been central to a notion of ritual purity. However the *varṇa* meaning of the ritual purity need not have been the same.

35. All tribal societies have a social organization based on kinship relations deriving from rules of exogamy and endogamy. Family structure, whether matrilineal or patriarchal, lineage and tribal identity are some of the features which might be ferreted out of the references to the earlier populations. Chalcolithic cultures invariably indicate a division of labour, and where there is trading activity as well, the division of labour is intensified. Nor would identity with a particular geographical location be precluded. The evidence of the notion of pollution in non-Aryanised societies has been noticed by anthropologists and some would regard it as essential to the development of religion and society in India (e.g. M. N. Srinivas, *Religion and Society among the Coorgs)*. Thus the pre-requisites for a caste structure as *jāti* with some ideological inputs could have been available. A rudimentary form of caste might have existed in the Ganga valley cultures and perhaps a better defined form in the Harappa culture. The Ṛgvedic people show an unfamiliarity with this structure which is not surprising if they regarded the non-Aryan culture as alien. The division of society into four groups has a single reference in the Puruṣasūkta hymn in the late tenth *maṇḍala* of the *Ṛgveda* (X.90.12). The logic implicit in this particular myth regarding the origin of the castes would in itself suggest the re-arranging of endogamous groups into a carefully worked-out pattern. The word *varṇa* with the connotation of caste is used in the *Ṛgveda* to differentiate between two groups, the *ārya* and the *dāsa*. The later literature clearly refers to the *catvāro varṇaḥ* (*Śatapatha Brāhmaṇa,* V.5.4.9; VI.4.4.13). Four categories would be necessary once society became more complex and endogamous groups were incorporated and had to be arranged in a pattern. The *jāti* structure may well reflect the substructure of caste.

36. e.g. *Chāndogya Upaniṣad,* V.10.7. Manu (X.45) makes a distinction between the Dasyus who speak the Aryan language and those who do not.

37. The Kirāta are referred to as low status tribes in the *Vājasaneyi Saṁhitā,* XXX.16; *Taittirīya Brāhmaṇa,* III.4.12.1; *Atharvaveda,* X.4.14; *Manu,* X.44; *Raghuvaṁśa,* XVI.57. The Pulinda are similarly referred to in the *Aitareya Brāhmaṇa*, 7.18; Aśoka's Thirteenth Major Rock Edict. J. Bloch, *Les Inscriptions d'Asoka*, Paris 1955, p. 125ff.

38. The urbanization of the Ganga valley in the first millennium BC is often referred to as the second urbanization. Crucial factors in this urbanization were new technologies such as iron, as is evident when one compares the NBPW levels with PGW levels or Black-and-Red Ware levels. Surplus produce and the specialization of crafts both utilizing the *dāsa-bhṛtaka,* increase in trade based on production as well as improved communication (both by land and through the use of river navigation) all combined to make urbanization possible. This in turn produced the characteristics associated with urban culture – the building of fortified cities, the introduction of a script *(brāhmī),* the use of coinage (punch-marked coins for example), a wide range of intellectual and metaphysical speculation (from the Cārvākas to the Ājīvikas), some of which reflected the requirements and aspirations of the new urban groups – the artisans and the merchants and traders.

Unlike the first urbanization in the Indus Valley, we have for the Ganga valley enough evidence to be able to trace its gradual evolution. The quality of the early urbanization of the Ganga valley as compared to that of the Indus valley was less impressive in terms of material culture. But there seems to have been a more even distribution of the characteristics of urbanization, suggesting perhaps that the perquisites of urban living were concentrated and centralized to a lesser degree than in the Indus civilisation.

39. The origin of the state is ascribed to a number of interesting factors in early literary sources. We are told, for example, that the surplus production of rice led to the emergence of the institution of family and private property (initially connoting fields). The state arose because of the need to prevent conflict. A deity appointed a ruler to govern. (*Vāyu Purāṇa*, VIII, 128–61; *Mārkaṇḍeya Purāṇa*, 49, 74ff). The literature referring to the late first millennium BC indicates the beginning of political concepts. This is in contrast to the Ṛgvedic period where loyalty is primarily to the clan and where, therefore, government is seen in more simplistic terms, namely, authority invested in the chief or leader whose main function is to protect the clan. This concept is 'assumed in the various stories regarding the appointment of Indra as the *rājā,* which stories are elaborated upon with the growth of

the contractual element in the notion of the state (*Ṛgveda,* VIII, 35, 86; *Aitareya Brāhmaṇa,* I.14; *Śatapatha Brāhmaṇa,* III.4.2.1–3). The purpose of the contract gradually changes from protecting the clan militarily, to the king maintaining the order of the castes and also protecting private property *(Arthaśāstra,* III.1; *Manu,* VII.17–35; *Śānti Parva,* 75.10; *Manu,* X.115). The contract is complete when the *rājā* is paid one-sixth in tax as his wage for services to the people *(ṣadbhāgbhṛto rājā rakṣet prajām, Baudhāyana Dharma Sūtra,* I.10.6). The *rājā* is associated with divinity which permits of a different perspective on the notion of contract.

Buddhist texts however indicate the contractual basis of the concept of the state, more clearly as the association with divinity is absent *(Dīgha Nikāya,* III, 84–96; *Mahāvastu,* I.338–48). It was more suited to the context of the non-monarchical systems of government.

40. At the level of ritual there was the incorporation of prayers, spells and magic, as for example in the *Atharvaveda* and the *Yajurveda.* At the level of deities the acceptance of the erstwhile distant Rudra and the growth of the Rudra-Śiva concept for instance. The recruitment of local priests into the *brāhmaṇa* fold can be seen not only in the various purification rites for those of degenerate castes, such as the *Vrātyastoma,* but is also perhaps reflected in the mysterious origin of many *brāhmaṇa gotras.* The concession to the worship of the mother goddess, to any appreciable extent, is a later phenomenon as also the acceptance of phallic worship. [D. D. Kosambi, 'On the Origin of the Brahmin *Gotras*', *Combined Methods in Indology*, pp. 98–166].

41. Pargiter's attempt to sort out the genealogies on the basis of Aryan and non-Aryan has been criticized. It is possible that, eventually, the Puranic genealogies will be found to be more true, not to the historicity but the essence of the history of this period, since they are not concerned with the Aryan problem as such but with the activities of a large number of clans and kings in northern India. It is interesting that the two royal lineages, the Ailas and Ikṣvākus are both based in the Ganga valley, from where various lineages move in various directions.

The *itihāsa-purāṇa* tradition has as its genesis the myth of the Flood and this agrees in many particulars with the Sumerian Flood legend. Indeed it is the agreement in details which is so striking. What is even more interesting is that the traditional date of the *kaliyuga* according to the astronomical tradition of Āryabhaṭa works out to about 3102 BC, which agrees with the archaeological date ascribed to the flooding of Shuruppak in Sumer which is probably the genesis of the Sumerian Flood legend (c. Leonard Woolley, *The Early Periods – Ur Excavations,* vol. IV, 1956; M. Mallowan, 'Noah's Flood Reconsidered', *Iraq,* XXVI, 1964). The reference to this legend in Vedic literature is late, in the *Śatapatha Brāhmaṇa,* 1.8.1.1 and the *Kāṭhaka Saṁhitā,* XI.2. Had the legend been of Aryan origin, one would expect it to occur in the *Ṛgveda* or be associated with the Avestan tradition rather than the Sumerian. The legend relating to the genesis of a people is after all of prime importance. Considering the close contacts between the Harappa culture and the Sumerians, it is possible that the same legend may have been used as a genesis in both cultures and the Puranic genealogies may therefore contain a pre-Aryan tradition. R.C. Hazra's very able studies of the Puranic sources point to some non-Vedic religious contents in the *Purāṇa*s.

As regards the mythological sections, the initial legend alone raises a host of interesting ideas: the concept of the Flood as genesis, the use of the sun and the moon as the symbol of the two royal lineages (Sūryavaṃśa and Candravaṃśa) and the association of these in the tribal mythology of India and elsewhere; the fact that the Aila lineage derives its name from the sole daughter of Manu, Iḷā who married the son of the moon deity (Soma), suggests a matrilineal-cum-mother goddess tradition.

42. Magadha in the period from 400 BC to AD 400 saw the rise of the Mauryas and the Guptas; the Raichur-Bijapur region in the period from 500 to 1200 AD was the nucleus of Cālukya and Rāṣṭrakūṭa power and the Kanchi-Tanjore region in the same period was the homeland of the Pallavas and Colas. Other areas also gave rise to important dynasties, but generally to only a single dynasty in a shorter period, e.g. Kannauj under Harṣa, Bengal under the Pālas, etc.

43. We know that various groups were recruited to the *brāhmaṇa varṇa* and that their status within the *varṇa* could change; thus the Kuru-Pāñcāla *brāhmaṇa*s looked down upon the Magadha *brāhmaṇa*s (*Jātaka,* I.324, II.83; *Aitareya Brāhmaṇa,* VIII.14), the Gāndhāra *brāhmaṇa*s are described with contempt in the *Rājataraṅgiṇī* (I.306ff) yet are regarded as respectable in the *Bhaviṣya Purāṇa*. It is also evident that families of non-kṣatriya origin became rulers or were given *kṣatriya* status through fabricated genealogies. Thus the Nandas are described as *śūdra*s in the *Purāṇa*s. The Candella kings claimed Candravaṃśi lineage and *kṣatriya* status in spite of obscure

origins and having acquired the status continued to marry into the local Gond families. There is an absence of any reference to the *vaiśya varṇa* in certain parts of India. The composition of the *śūdra varṇa* varied from region to region and its role was different in south India as compared to the Ganga valley. When we cease to look at early Indian society as a static, rigid structure stratified into immobile castes, we then begin to see evidence to suggest the contrary.

4.

THE ṚGVEDA

ENCAPSULATING SOCIAL CHANGE[1]

I

Aryan domination, irrespective of form or agency, has been the basic theme of the history of the first millennium BC in India. This was said to be the result of either an invasion or a migration into India of people belonging to the Aryan race in such numbers that it resulted in a displacement of pre-existing populations and their primitive cultures. The latter were said to have fled to the south of the sub-continent, where they came to be called the Dravidian race, a Dravidian culture. The invasion was said to be of a superior race of Aryans who subjugated the autochthons, reduced them to slavery and introduced civilization.

This view was useful to colonial interpretations of Indian history since parallels were drawn between the Aryan conquest and the British conquest. It also appealed to some members of the upper castes who saw themselves as the lineal, biological descendants of the racially superior Aryans. Nationalist historiography by and large accepted the theory of invasion. Some who were not historians preferred to think of the Aryans as indigenous in order to claim Indian origins for what was regarded as a superior civilization.

As an interesting reversal, it also became a major argument in the claim of lower castes who maintained that the *brāhmaṇa*s were alien invaders and oppressors and had usurped the rights to the land of the indigenous lower castes, Dalits and tribals.[2] This view sought support from the discovery of the Indus Civilization as the pre-Aryan civilization of the indigenous peoples. The Aryan theory therefore has been central to many of the political contestations over identity and status during the evolution of the Indian nation-state in the last two centuries. As a contrast to this, although Aryanisation is assumed in some pre-colonial sources, it is rarely defined or analyzed in detail.

The theory of an invasion has now been discarded. It was originally based on references in the *Ṛgveda* to hostilities between the *ārya*s and the *dāsa*s, taken as representations of the victorious Aryans overcoming the local Dasas. It has been replaced by theories favouring small-scale migrations. These may have been the cause of the skirmishes between various groups and for a variety of reasons. Nevertheless, the establishing of the Indo-Aryan language did not require conflictual situations.

However, the pendulum has also swung to the other extreme among some archaeologists and historians and it is now being said that not only were the Aryans indigenous but that they were also the authors of the Indus Civilization (renamed by them as the Indus–Sarasvatī civilization) and that the *Ṛgveda* as the earliest composition of the Aryans should be identified with the Harappa Culture of the third millennium BC or even the pre-Harappa Culture of the fourth millennium.[3] Despite the constant repetition of this view in an attempt to enforce it, it fails the test, since the evidence – both archaeological and literary – does not support it.[4] This is a different argument from that which suggests that there could have been some elements of continuity from Harappan times into the later period and that the Vedic culture as a post-Harappan culture may reflect an occasional example. The notion that the Vedic culture and language had a genesis entirely within the Indian subcontinent goes back to a few colonial views, but substantially to the politically motivated Hindutva literature of the 1920s and 1930s. The intention was to insist that the Hindus alone, as lineal descendants of the Aryans, were indigenous, whereas the Muslims and Christians were alien. The Dalit insistence that the Aryan invasion resulted in caste confrontation, as had been proposed by Jyotiba Phule, was replaced in the Hindutva view by identifying differences on the basis of religion. Needless to say it makes little historical sense to speak of identities as indigenous or alien for a period three thousand years ago, when there were no cartographic boundaries or national territories, and there were immense intermixtures of peoples, and considerable cultural heterogeneity. At most, origins of predominant traits can be located.

In any comparison of the Harappan and Ṛgvedic cultures it is necessary to consider their parameters and their systemic patterns, and not limit the discussion to what might be a few items familiar to each. The Harappa Culture cannot be identified with the Ṛgvedic as they are neither contemporary nor are their characteristics identical. The geographical area included in the Harappan system was far more extensive than the region known to the *Ṛgveda*.

The Indus Civilization had an extensive agrarian base and an urban population dependent on food production in rural areas. Huge storage structures have been identified possibly as granaries or as warehouses. Not only was it essentially urban but the construction of structures in the elite sections of the cities involved massive brick platforms which, apart from extensive brick-making, would have required elaborate arrangements for obtaining and controlling labour. This implies an entirely different social organization from that characteristic of the *Ṛgveda*. The demarcation between the citadel area of the elite and the residential area was emphasized by a physical separation and the latter consisted of large familial houses with well-developed civic amenities. The lay-out of the cities and the meticulously constructed drainage system are pointers to a sophisticated urbanism. This suggests a system more advanced than that of clan chiefdoms.

The economy of the cities was based on the gathering of resources and the production of items for trade such as beads and copper ingots among others. The technology of copper-bronze was not spectacular but focused on a range of items. Obtaining raw materials and organizing craft production would have required a substantial category of supervisors and managers. A script, (as yet undeciphered), was widely employed and was functional in origin. For instance, one of the uses of the seals on which it occurs was for stamping packages of goods. Little is known of the Harappan religion and the possibility of fertility cults and mother-goddess worship has been postulated. The animals most frequently depicted on the seals are the 'unicorn' – perhaps a version of the rhinoceros, and the bull, the elephant and occasionally the tiger.[5] The horse is conspicuously absent until the early second millennium BC when stray horse bones turn up as they do in west Asia. Associated with the horse was the chariot and the spoked wheel, both as innovations.

The gradual decay of the cities, generally attributed to environmental factors and decline in trade, did not result in the termination of the culture. There is evidence of the usual characteristics of declining urban centres – squatters and rural migrants moving in, and a dispersal of the city population. There were contacts not only with subsequent cultures such as the Painted Grey Ware in some sites of the Punjab, but possibly also with contemporary Black and Red Ware sites in Gujarat. It is feasible to suggest that some of the Harappan tradition probably in the form of mythology and rituals may well have continued. Nevertheless the decline of the cities would have resulted in a discontinuance of the Harappan administrative system and in the rural areas people would have been unprotected and subject to new forms of dominance by local authorities. It may legitimately be asked if there was now a search for new protectors.

The *Ṛgveda* describes a non-urban, chalcolithic, agro-pastoral society with cattle keeping as its central concern. The geographical spread of the *Ṛgveda* is only a part of the much larger area involved in the Indus civilisation. Areas crucial to the Harappan trade such as Gujarat, Sind, Oman, the Persian Gulf and Mesopotamia are unknown to the *Ṛgveda,* whose geography has been defined by the rivers listed in the late *nadī-stuti* hymn (10.75),[6] essentially eastern Afghanistan and the undivided Punjab upto the water-shed. The geography of the Vedic corpus subsequent to the *Ṛgveda* and incorporating the Ganga valley is of course outside the experience of the Indus civilization.

There is little in the *Ṛgveda* about craft production, the main concern being with cattle-raids and the produce of cattle herds. The metal technology of the *Ṛgveda* is copper-bronze, the metal being referred to as *ayas* (6.3.5; 47.10). There might have been some veering towards iron since the meaning of the generic word *ayas* could refer to iron, even if the latter is generally described in the post-Ṛgvedic corpus as the dark metal – *kṛṣṇa ayas*. A writing system has no function in this culture. The rhinoceros, elephant and tiger are unfamiliar animals. The horse however is central to socio-economic functioning – in herding, raiding and transportation – and to ritual as the focus of a major sacrifice – which was to evolve into the *aśvamedha*. The authors of the *Ṛgveda* are critical of the rites pertaining to fertility cults and the reference to goddesses are few and far between. The Ṛgvedic religion is dominated by male deities among whom Indra is pre-eminent.

This brief summary should clarify the essentially different type of societies that emerge from the evidence of the Harappa Culture and the *Ṛgveda,* even if there may be some small similarity in a few items. To argue therefore that the *Ṛgveda* should be identified with the Harappa Culture points to a lack in understanding the essentials of the comparative method in historical analysis.

II

The linguistic evidence for Vedic Sanskrit as an Indo-Aryan language and therefore part of the Indo-European family, is overwhelming.[7] This includes the fact that Indo-Aryan and Old Iranian are cognates. Therefore, the evidence from the *Avesta* and particularly the earlier part of the *Avesta,* the *Gāthā*s, such as names, locations and concepts, has also to be discussed in the context of early Vedic studies. A few Indo-Aryan names of deities and technical terms for training horses occur in inscriptions further west in northern Syria and Anatolia, dating to the mid-second millennium BC. Archaeologically there are no links between this area and north India. These fragments are thought to belong to an earlier Proto-Indo-Aryan group connected with central Asia.[8] The Indo-Aryan language appears to have arrived in India from north eastern Iran and Afghanistan in the second millennium BC. This is paralleled by the presence of similar languages at a similar time in west Asia.

The language of the Harappan script has not yet been deciphered. Those that play a guessing game try to read it as Indo-Aryan, but the more systematic linguistic analyses seem to suggest Proto-Dravidian.[9] An early form of Munda has also been considered.[10] That there was a substantial presence of non-Aryan languages, particularly Dravidian and Austro-Asiatic, in northern India is now well-attested and is evident from the incorporation of elements from these languages into Vedic Sanskrit. These increase in the later *Veda*s. They are noticeably absent in other parallel languages in west Asia.[11] Given this linguistic evidence, the historically significant question is of determining the process by which Indo-Aryan was introduced into northern India and the manner in which it gradually became the dominant language despite the presence of other languages.[12] This is in turn tied to analyzing the relationship between speakers of different languages, the intersections of these relationships with socio-economic status and the gradual evolution of dominant groups and subordinated groups. This essay is addressed to these questions using the *Ṛgveda* as its source. Attempts to address these issues move away from simplistic explanations such as massive invasions, overwhelming migrations or even the static situation of their being indigenous peoples. Instead the attempt is to investigate historical and cultural processes in societies that experience change and are not static.

The initial closeness and subsequent separation of the speakers of Indo-Aryan from those who spoke Old Iranian is characterized by a similarity of some terms and a deliberate reversal of some concepts. Thus the *airiia* and *dāha* of the *Avesta* are the *ārya* and *dāsa* of the *Ṛgveda;* and *asura* originally a term of veneration in the early *Ṛgveda* eventually becomes a reference to the demonic and has the opposite meaning to its cognate *ahura* in Avestan. It is thought that there were likely to have been modifications by migrants coming from Iran and from what are now called the Indo-Iranian borderlands, to north-western India. These were small scale migrations in low gear, of groups looking for new lands in which to settle. They were likely to have been movements of clans fissioning off owing to competitive conditions or disagreements, as frequently happens. The Indo-Aryan speakers gradually established themselves in north-western India. There are some links suggested by the archaeology of the second millennium BC between these areas and Bactria and Margiana in Afghaṇistan and Iran.[13] These are other than the obvious links of the appearance of the horse, the chariot and the spoked wheel at sites in north-western India. The *Ṛgveda,* as a collection of hymns composed in the latter half of the mid-second millennium BC, is an articulation of this process.

The *Ṛgveda* was read by nineteenth century scholars as demonstrating racial conflict: the conflict between the *ārya* and *dāsa varṇa*s, the fair-skinned Aryans invading and subjugating the dark-skinned *dāsa*s. Skin pigmentation came to be the accepted meaning of the term *varṇa* and was foundational to a racial explanation of what was viewed as the beginnings of Indian history, as is evident from nineteenth century opinions such as those of Max Müller, and others. The racial difference was then extended to include flat noses and the nose became a significant feature of ethnographic indices relating to race.[14] This meaning of *varṇa* was used in colonial theories of caste which explained it as a system of organizing racial segregation. However prior to European studies of the *Ṛgveda,* no racial connotation was associated with *varṇa*. The description of caste as based on racial segregation encouraged an avoidance in discussing discrimination based on access to and control of resources and wealth, control over labour, and/or the function of ritual, and other such considerations.

However *ārya* is a linguistic, social and cultural marker and even if there is occasional mention of physical differentiation this does not amount to a racial identity. In the process of societies and cultures adjusting to each other, the term *ārya* fairly quickly lost whatever ethnic connotation it may have had. The centrality of speech, and correct speech at that, became a social marker and was doubtless also linked to the supposed efficacy of *mantra*s, of which it is repeatedly stated that the sound has to be precise and faultless for the *mantra* to be effective. Yet even within the history of Vedic Sanskrit the exemplar of correct speech changed through the incorporation of elements from other languages. The *Ṛgveda* therefore is not a document describing the *ārya*s as closing ranks through claims to biological and racial descent. On the contrary it is likely that it was possible for some people to gradually acquire *ārya* status, through a familiarity with Indo-Aryan and through practicing the cultural and ritual norms of those who had the status of *āryas*: a process not unfamiliar to subsequent social history. The hymns do not present a monolithic *ārya* identity in confrontation with a monolithic *dāsa* identity. There is both a range of groups within and between the *ārya* and the *dāsa,* and a flexibility in identity. The collection of hymns therefore assumes the presence of a number of societies and peoples with varied relationships.

Locations mentioned in the *Ṛgveda* indicate a familiarity with eastern Afghanistan as well as towards the Indo-Gangetic watershed. The *nadī-stuti* hymn in a late section of the *Ṛgveda* sets the final geographical frame as being between the north-west and the watershed *(Ṛgveda* 10.75). Contacts with north eastern Iran and Afghanistan also go back over a long period. It is unlikely that the inhabitants of the Punjab would have viewed the Indo-Iranian borderlands as either distant or alien. The area has historically always played the role of the intermediary land between Afghanistan and Central Asia and the Ganga plain, and allowing for a little exaggeration one could use the analogy of its being a toggle-switch between what were later powerful states in Iran and India. The coming and going of families and migrants, whether as pastoralists, traders, caravaneers, missionaries or as armies, has been a constant feature since antiquity of the history of the north west.

It is interesting that there is information in the *Ṛgveda* on rivers but little on other geographical features such as mountains or for that matter, place names. Familiarity with rivers would point to the search for pastures, sources of water and arable land along river banks. River courses changed necessitating the movement of peoples and these would most likely have followed the rivers.

Characteristic of those living in this area in the late second and early first millennium was that these were cultures of small settlements with recognisable differences. The Indo-Iranian borderlands, the Swat valley, Punjab and the confluence of the Indus system provide a number of distinctively different archaeological cultures. The Gandhara Grave Culture in the Swat valley introduces the horse and iron technology in the late second and early first millennium BC, and some would argue that these were due to links with Bactria and Margiana. Sites such as Gumla in the Gomal valley and Periano Guṅdai in the Zhob valley point to disturbed conditions but only locally. Pirak in the Bolan valley also has evidence of the horse but only in the early second millennium BC. The Cemetery H culture with some new features such as in the decoration of burial urns, had a short duration in a limited area. Settlements in the Cholistan area were deserted with a migration to the watershed. There was therefore not just one entry point into the north-west but many and the movement of peoples within the region was in diverse directions.

The Indo-Gangetic watershed and the western Ganga plain were host to cultures of the Ochre Colour Pottery and the Painted Grey Ware.[15] More widely scattered are the cultures of the Black-and-Red Ware, in Rajasthan and Gujarat, at the fringes of the Punjab and the *Doāb,* and of a later date in the middle Ganga plain. These cultures are not suggestive of an authoritative, uniform, control. None were dominant cultures as compared for instance to the Harappan, but nevertheless they had a noticeable presence. The authors of the *Ṛgveda* were not functioning in uninhabited territories and the existing populations were not primitive autochthons but Chalcolithic societies of agro-pastoralists and agriculturalists with a defined culture. The archaeological data reflect the cultural presence of multiple groups and practices.

The Iranian *Avesta* had some notions of a homeland, even if mythical and called it the Airiianem Vaejo,[16] but this is not referred to in the *Ṛgveda*. Given that Old Iranian and Indo-Aryan were cognates, the homeland referred to in the *Avesta* could extend to include the Indo-Aryan speakers as well. Homelands become particularly important at times of insecurity and dissension, as was presumably the case in Iran if there was a breaking away of what became the Indo-Aryan speakers. Significantly the *Ṛgveda* does not refer to the *āryas* being of common blood. The hymns have diverse authors and refer to events and situations which need not always have been contemporary. Various clans and chiefs are mentioned, alliances are made or broken and hostilities are not consistently between the same groups. The hymns provide evidence of clan movement and of settlements in various parts of the north-west and the Punjab.

Movement involves migrations and these are recorded. We are told of clans crossing rivers and coming from afar.[17] The mention of the Sarasvatī and the Sarayū in the early sections of the *Ṛgveda* have been associated more logically by some scholars with Haraxvaiti and Harayu in Afghanistan. The Sarayū is mentioned thrice and even in the late section it is linked with the rivers of the north west (5.53.9; 4.30.18; 10.64.9). The name Sarayū in present day Uttar Pradesh is historically much later. The river name Gomatī also travels from the north west to the Ganga valley in a later period. This points to distance and association. Conflicts with *dāsas* such as Śambara and Varcin in the mountainous regions have been placed in the north-west (4.30.14; 2.14.6; 2.12.11; 6.47.21). Indra helped by attacking the *purs* of the *dāsas* and thus creating space for the *āryas* (2.20.7). This is reminiscent of the creating of new lands for the migrating *airiias* in the *Avesta*.[18] Migration in the *Avesta* is explained by overpopulation and pressure on the land, which has to continually expand itself – even if miraculously – to accomodate more people and larger herds.

Migrations did not preclude the occasional violent confrontation although localized. Some were among the clans that identified themselves as *āryas*, and some were between them and others. The Bharatas were set upon by the ten clans, on the Paruṣṇī or Ravi river (7.18). Elsewhere it is said that Indra helps them cross the Vipāś/Beas and the Śutudrī/Satluj (3.33.11ff). This would suggest an eastward migration towards the watershed. Despite being among the more important clans, the Bharatas are not associated with coming from very far away. The closely linked Yadu and Turvaśa clans came from far and had to cross many large rivers swollen with floods, which they did with help from Indra. He saved them from drowning as he did many others (1.131.5; 1.174.9; 4.30.17; 6.45.1; 6.20.12; 2.13.12). The crossing of rivers would be expected in the terrain of the borderlands and the Punjab.

The Yadus were associated with the Pārśavas, identified by some scholars with the Persians/Iranians (8.6.46). The Pūrus too helped by Indra eventually won land and success (7.19.3) as did some others. The Maruts are called upon to help in crossing the waters and arriving at good lands (7.56.24; 5.53.9). For Indra the floods are stilled in the seven streams thus helping the heroes to get across (8.85.1). Indra leads the clans of the *ārya*s across regions difficult to traverse (6.22.7). These migrations seem to support the likelihood of the Indo-Aryan speakers breaking away from Iran. That Indra helps the migrants might also support the contention of the *Avesta* in its delineation of Indra as demoniac, and opposed to the benevolent Iranian deity, Ahura Mazda, for it would seem that the worshippers of Indra migrated away from Iran.

A later text, the *Śrautasūtra* of Baudhāyana locates various clans of the post-Ṛgvedic period and the locations suggest clan movements. The clans are said to be kin-related. Some clans which are the descendents of Āyu are located to the east in the watershed and the Ganga plain such as the Kuru-Pañcālas and the Kāśi-Videhas; and some who are the descendents of his brother Amāvasa are located in the Indo-Iranian borderlands to the west such as the Gandhāra, Pārśava and Araṭṭa.[19] Interestingly the latter remained permanently in the borderlands and the north-west with which they are associated in later periods as well, and their cultures are connected to those even further west. The Videhas on the other hand are recorded (in other texts) as having migrated from the watershed considerably eastwards to the middle Ganga plain.

The new land although spacious, has inadequacies. There is almost a fear of the land being too narrow and hedged in, reminiscent of the Avestan description of the earth before its frequent and necessary expansion. There is a longing to settle in broad alluvial lands rather than in narrow pastures.[20] The new lands are said to be narrow and the country pathless (6.47.20-21). Narrowness, is contrasted with expansiveness and the gods are prayed to for protection against being hemmed in (8.18.5-6; 2.23.18). Skirmishes associated with the inroads of clans into new areas (2.13.8; 2.14.7; 1.53.9-10; 6.18.3) tend to be exaggerated, sometimes highly so, a characteristic of much heroic poetry. Yet there were raids and skirmishes requiring constant appeals to Indra for overcoming the *dāsa*s and others. But this was not widespread warfare or conquest on a large scale. Since river courses had a tendency to shift, pastures and fields would also be affected. The search for fresh pastures could well have resulted in skirmishes. Had these been clans long established in the area, changing river courses would not have posed such immense problems.

Coming to a new land is also indicated by the need to invent or borrow names for new plants and animals. Domesticated rice for example is known from excavations in Sind in Harappan times and the Doāb in the early first millennium BC and even earlier further east, but is unfamiliar to the *Ṛgveda* and does not appear to be included in the general term for grain, *yava*. Sanskrit words for the rhinoceros do not occur in the *Ṛgveda* but occur at a later date and are also said to be non Indo-Aryan by some linguists. The much-quoted reference to the elephant as *mṛga hastin* (1.64.7; 4.16.14), literally, the animal with a hand, points to an unfamiliarity with the animal so frequently depicted on Harappan seals. Another intriguing aspect is that the *Ṛgveda* refers to *siṃha*/lion but not to *vyāghra*/tiger. The power, majesty, roar and strength of the lion are invoked particularly in the early sections of the *Ṛgveda* (9.97.28; 5.15.3; 3.9.4; 5.74.4; 5.83.3). It is unlikely that there would have been confusion between the lion and the tiger since they are distinctively different. The difference is recognized in the *vyāghra* being mentioned later in the *Atharvaveda,* generally given a more easterly locale in the Ganga valley. Whereas the tiger is frequently depicted on the Harappan seals, the lion is absent. It is thought that the earlier habitat of the lion was further west in Iran. A Mesopotamian seal depicting a man grappling with a lion on either side is repeated in the Indus Civilization but the lions are substituted by tigers. The horse on the other hand is not only an animal of central importance, but the Indo-Aryan for the horse – *aśva-* has cognates in Indo-European.[21]

III

Any discussion of the societies described in the *Ṛgveda* inevitably involves the identification of the *ārya* and the *dāsa,* for this dichotomy has coloured the reconstruction of the history of this period and the reading of later times as well. Differing from the *ārya*s are not only the *dāsa*s, but also the *rākṣasa*s, the *paṇi*s, and eventually the *asura*s. The last of these is an ambiguous category with a change in the qualities associated with them where they finally emerge evoking evil and magical powers.[22] They are in turn distinct from the *yātudhāna*/sorcerers upon whom the wrath of the gods is called (1.133.3; 1.191.8; 7.104.15; 9.71.1; 10.87.8; 8.35.18; 9.86.48; 10.118.8). This essay is however limited to discussing the relationship between the *ārya*s and the *dāsa*s.

There has been considerable discussion over the definition of *ārya*. In the nineteenth century it was taken to mean a race and equated with language. Subsequently, there has been a teasing out of its meaning to an enemy/friend, a stranger, a companion, a hospitable one, or a person of status and wealth.[23] These latter meanings negate the racial connotation. Nevertheless, it is surprising how frequently the racial connotation is either implicit or explicit in both scholarly and popular writing on 'the Aryans'.

The concept of an Aryan race has now been discarded, as indeed have attempts to equate language with race.[24]

It can be argued that in the *Ṛgveda, ārya* designates a particular group of people, sometimes also referred to as the *ārya varṇa* (e.g. 3.34.9), and there are occasional references to the *dāsa varṇa* as well (e.g. 2.12.4). This has led in the past to a dichotomizing of the two into uniform, monolithic, confrontational groups based on a racial identity. Both formulations are questionable. The differentiation emphasized in the *Ṛgveda* is a distinction based on language, ritual observances and custom. The distinction between those who spoke the language correctly and coherently and those who did not is significant, for the latter are described by the epithet *mṛdhra vāc*. This distinction became central in the Vedic corpus to the definition of the *mleccha*s who spoke incorrectly[25] and who later also did not observe the *varṇāśramadharma,* the regulations of *varṇa* society, and were therefore treated as impure and outside the social pale.[26] *Ārya* therefore would more correctly be a social and linguistic qualifier rather than a racial category.

The term *ārya* is used in various grammatical forms which would not be the case if it were essentially a racial label (1.117.21; 3.34.9; 10.65.11; 6.22.10; 7.83.1). It is used for gods as well when Indra is said to be like an *ārya* leading away a *dāsa,* which could suggest status rather than race (5.34.6). There is little specific indication as to who is the *ārya* and the frequency of references to the *āryas* are about half in number as compared to *dāsa* and *dasyu*. This is different from the *Avesta* where the *airiia* is specified and is the most frequently mentioned. The authors of the hymns mention both their *ārya* and *dāsa* enemies.

In the past, the racial identification of *ārya* and *dāsa* has been made largely on the basis of the use of *varṇa* as a division of peoples and reference to *tvacam kṛṣṇām* as black-skinned people. The literal meaning of *varṇa* is colour or cover, but it is used generally in the *Ṛgveda* in the sense of colour, namely, the colours and the hues of dawn, the day, night, clouds, and so on. Its use with *ārya* and *dāsa* however is likely to have been more as a symbol of duality or social division rather than of skin pigmentation. Mention is made of *asuryam varṇam,* which is cast off in the course of the preparation of Soma (9.71.2). The later *Śatapatha Brāhmaṇa* mentions a variety of *varṇas*.[27]

As a cultural contrast, white and black is common to early Indian metaphors, such as in relation to *pakṣa* – the fortnights of a month, or the Black and White *Yajurveda,* and so on. Other interpretations of *varṇa* have also been suggested. For example, *varṇa* may be taken as contrasting cosmic moieties.[28] Prajāpati created *deva*s and *asura*s as representing two cosmic moieties, where *deva*s are described as the white colour of the day, and *asura*s as the black colour of the night. It is interesting that these are the two cosmic moieties mentioned in the *Avesta,* except that there the *ahura*s have precedence over the *daeva*s. Colour is not always to be taken literally as frequently it is symbolic of qualities and attributes.

One of the epithets of those that are disliked is *tvacam kṛṣṇām,* and because it is used in the same verse which refers to the *dāsa*s being *avrata* or without laws and rites (1.130.8), and by implication not observing the rites of the *ārya*s, it is said to refer to the *dāsa*s. Does the black skin here identify the *dāsa?* Renou in his discussion of this verse, separates those without laws and those that are black-skinned.[29] Could the black skin refer to the condition of those not observing the rites, after they have been burnt by Indra which this verse so graphically describes? The fourteenth century commentator on the *Veda*s, Sāyaṇa, explains *tvacam kṛṣṇām* as referring to an *asura* named Kṛṣṇa, whose skin was torn to pieces by Indra. It is also curious that the one reference which could suggest a dark skin pigmentation of some of the *dāsa*s occurs in the later section of the *Ṛgveda*. Surely if skin pigmentation was so striking and the description was being contrasted with the fair skin of the *ārya*s, then such an obvious physical difference would be mentioned unambiguously and frequently in the earliest sections of the *Ṛgveda*. Most of the descriptions using the epithet *kṛṣṇa* or dark, occur in ambiguous forms which allow of readings different from skin pigmentation.

Three other references are cited to suggest a dark skin pigmentation but these again have been interpreted differently. *Kṛṣṇagarbhāḥ* does not refer to *dāsa*s or *dasyu*s specifically and black here could as well mean pregnant with evil or the dark (1.101.1).[30] Geldner translates it as "Schwarzen Schwangeren" or black foetuses.[31] Renou translates it as having in their womb the black, and adds "race" in brackets.[32] He relates it to another term, *kṛṣṇayoniḥ,* which he renders as " noirs embryons" black embryos. This term, often taken as the black womb has been translated by both Griffith and Geldner as dwelling – *yona* – in darkness (2.20.7 and cf. 1.63.4), perhaps suggesting the darkness of the womb. The identity of those being attacked in the smiting of the fifty thousand dark ones, is again unclear (4.16.13). There is also a mention of *kṛṣṇām tvacam* in association with the processing of *soma* which could refer to the black ox-hides used in the process and need not be taken for the skin pigmentation of the *dāsa* (9.41.1). The subsequent verse speaks of quelling the *dasyu* because of his being without rites. References to driving away the black/dark ones have to be read carefully as often the context is that of nights being driven away by days or clouds being driven away by the sun. The swarthy skin which Indra dislikes, the *asiknim* or the not-white, does not specifically qualify *dāsas* even though *avratān* is mentioned (9.73.5). Sāyaṇa reads it as the swarthy skin blown away from the earth by a celestial power and suggests that it is the going away of the darkness of the night (4.17.4). In some instances, *tvacam* seems to be used in the sense of a covering over the earth (10.68.4).

Was *kṛṣṇa* therefore used invariably to mean a dark/black skin or was it used metaphorically to mean black as evil or as associated with "the Other"? There could well have been some groups of dark-skinned people but were they necessarily the *dāsas,* and is the *ārya–dāsa* distinction based largely on skin colour indicating racial identities, or is this view the result of nineteenth century pre-occupations with race? There is in any case a difference between the observance of skin colour in societies of the past and the interpretation of this as racial identities, given that racial distinctions are a recent idea in history. In the three cases referred to above, *kṛṣṇa* could be read as meaning evil rather than black of skin. White and black is a common dichotomy used in many cultural contexts. It also occurs with a reversal of association, in the phrase, "the brood of darkness", which is a description of the *daeva*s, the hostile people in the *Avesta* and not the *dāsa*s, and the context makes it clear that darkness refers to evil and not to skin colour.[33]

If the *dāsa*s were dark skinned then by contrast the *ārya*s should have been fair or white skinned. But the *ārya* is not described as such. The word *śveta*/white, is used in association with *soma,* Vāyu, horses, bulls, goats and vessels, but not human pigmentation. There is one reference to Indra and his white fair friends and this again may have nothing to do with complexion as has been translated by various translators, for Sāyaṇa provides the best explanation: that it refers to the dazzling brightness of the Maruts who are Indra's companions. Mention of the swarthy fifty thousand, again not clearly identified as *dāsa*s, is read by Sāyaṇa as the evil *rākṣasa*s (4.16.13).

Conflicts among those assumed to be *ārya*s are also mentioned. A confrontation is referred to in which a confederacy of ten *rājā*s attacked Sudās and Indra came to his aid (7.18.7). This was not a pitched battle nor was it between *āryas* and *dāsa*s. It would seem that the enemies of Sudās tried to break the banks of the river or change its course. Conflict over the control of river water would not be surprising in an agro-pastoral society. Sudās was assisted by the Tṛtsus and they were all companions, although elsewhere it is suggested that the Tṛtsus with their white robes and braided hair were proficient in chanting and in the worship of Indra, which doubtless was taken as a contribution to the victory (7.83.8). But on another occasion Indra helped two of the ten, Turvaśa and Yadu (4.30.17). Indra, sometimes helps to subordinate *dāsa* chiefs to *ārya* control but on other occasions is hostile to some *āryas* (1.53.10; 6.18.13; 2.11.19-20; 4.30.18). Sudās had both *dāsa* and *ārya* enemies (7.83.1). Sometimes the *ārya* and the *dāsa* are mentioned as symmetrical enemies of the authors of the hymns (6.22.10; 6.33.3; 6.60.6; 10.69.6; 10.83.1; 10.86.19; 10.102.3). They do not appear to be self-contained, discrete entities. The hatred of both the *dāsa* and the *ārya* has to be quelled and their weapons kept away (10.102.3). Such references seem to increase in the last *maṇḍala* and one wonders whether this reflects a sharpening of the perception of the relationship.

The *dāsas* are said to have their own *viś*/clan (6.25.2; 2.11.4; 4.28.4) but their clan names are not given although *dāsa* chiefs are named. Many *dāsas,* as for example Śambara, are associated with mountains suited to the topography of the borderlands. This is also suggested by the use of the term *dāsa* doubtless associated with the Avestan *daha*. Were both the terms *ārya* and *dāsa* being used in a generic sense for those of better status wishing to subordinate the others? Conflict with the *dāsas* is mainly to raid their strongholds and loot their wealth, generally cattle and where possible horses as well. Cattle-wealth could move along with the raiders. Pastoralists would want to maintain the optimum size of their herds. Travelling through mountainous terrain and crossing flooded rivers may have depleted the animal numbers. The raid, if successful, was also a rapid form of acquiring wealth. The *dāsa*s are described as wealthy and are said to hide their treasure, their cattle and gold.

On one occasion the conflict is over *kṛṣṭi*, which may have been arable land (6.18.3), but most often the prize consists of animal herds, which are also the prime gifts to the bards.[34] Frequent mention is made of Indra and Agni shattering the *pur*s of the *dāsa*s (1.103.3; 4.26.3; 4.30.13). When there is a metaphorical reference to the *dāsa*s or to the dark-hued, the numbers are exaggeratedly large such as 30,000, 50,000, 6666, 100,000 and 5, or hundreds of thousands, and it is not clear whether these are specific to the *dāsa*s or merely a general reference to enemies (2.13.8-9; 4.30.21; 6.26.2–5). The identity of the authors of the hymns vis-a-vis the *ārya* and the *dāsa* is somewhat submerged in their applauding the patron who is generous. They pray to Indra for wealth and for subduing with his help and with that of the *āryas* all the *dasyu*s (2.11.19).

What seems to emerge especially in the later hymns, is that although the *ārya* and the *dāsa varṇa*s are opposed to each other, nevertheless in each category there are those who do not conform to a clear-cut opposition, such as the Pūrus among the *āryas* and Balbūtha among the *dāsa*s. There is far more ambiguity in these identities than has been conceded in the past. Those specifically referred to as *ārya*s are fewer than others left undefined which would be compatible with *ārya* being a term for high status rather than a racial identity.

There appears to have been a differentiation of categories among both groups where some *āryas* are also not observing the laws and patronizing the rituals. The Pūrus are sometimes described with the epithet *mṛdhra vāc* suggesting their inability to master the language of the *ārya* (7.18.13) and yet on occasion they are favoured by Indra (1.130.7). This is also the pattern with the Turvaśas and the Yadus who are saved by Indra in crossing rivers but are enemies of Sudās who was befriended by Indra (4.30.17; 7.18.6). But Indra is hostile to the Druhyus who, according to later *Purāṇas*, may even have been the kinsmen of the above three.

It has been argued that if the migrations were in multiple waves then those who came in the earliest phase would be speaking a language not identical with that of those who came later. Thus *mṛdhra vāc* would not invariably indicate a *dāsa* but could also refer to those of *ārya* status who nevertheless spoke a Sanskrit regarded as faulty by the latest arrivals. The case of the Pūrus however seems to be one of a social mutation, since the epithet of *mṛdhra vāc* is used for them in an early section of the *Ṛgveda* and it is also stated in one of the later *Brāhmaṇa*s that Pūru had an *asura rākṣasa* ancestry. Not all those to whom Indra is hostile are necessarily *dāsa*s (1.51.8).

Some clans are more ancient than others and call for greater respect. The Bharatas are closely related to the worship of fire (6.16.4) and Agni is given the title of Bharata (2.7.1; 4.25.4; 6.16.19). That the Bharatas were an established clan with impressive antecedents is suggested by the fact that a potted genealogy of five or six generations can be constructed for them from the *Ṛgveda,* suggesting a higher status. Even this depth of genealogy was not common among most other clans.

The Pūrus are said to have dwelt on the two grassy banks of the Sarasvatī (7.96.1-2), and the attack on Sudās was to capture the waters at some point on the Ravi with perhaps better lands. If the early references to the Sarasvatī are to the Haraxvaiti in Afghanistan, then the conflict could have been over a move from the borderlands to the plains. The latter presumably provided access to better pastures, better stubble fields and closer links with cultivators and would have changed social and political patterns. If the Sarasvatī had in fact been the Hakra it was by now unlikely to have grassy banks, and even if new pastures were needed, then the logical move would have been in the direction of the watershed where others had gone previously and settled, rather than the reverse direction of going northwards to what was obviously a congested area involving a major conflict.

The Pūrus joined the confederacy of the ten against the Bharatas. But this did not prevent Indra from helping them on other occasions, even to destroy settlements and win land (1.130.7; 6.20.10; 7.19.3) despite their being described as *mṛdhra vāc* (7.18.13) and later, being said to be of *asura rākṣasa* ancestry.[35] Who the land is won from is not stated. In the subsequent period, the Bharatas, the Tṛtsus and the Pūrus were to form an alliance leading to the confederacy of the Kurus. Located in the upper Doāb and the eastern watershed this was to be described as the land of the finest Sanskrit, presumably superceding the earlier form used in the Punjab.[36] That the Sanskrit of a particular region is singled out as the best, indicates the presence of dialects, and interestingly the recommended later forms had an admixture from languages that were not Indo-Aryan.

The terms *dāsa* and *dasyu* are on occasion used interchangeably suggesting that the difference was minor if at all (4.28.4; 4.30.14; 5.30.9; 6.26.5; 6.31.4; 10.22.8). The hostility to *dasyu*s seems more because of their not performing the correct rites. Both categories were people whose ways were alien and therefore liable to be regarded with contempt, but at the same time they were feared, since a large number of hymns to Indra and Agni in particular, are prayers for help in subduing the *dāsa*s so that their wealth could be appropriated. The prayers are so urgent and insistent that it would seem that the *dāsa*s were difficult to subdue. Did this eventually require some compromises towards the erstwhile *dāsa*s? Those *dāsa*s, earlier seen as 'the Other', may now, where they commanded the language and had status and wealth, have begun to participate in the evolving of the society of the *ārya,* i.e., those claiming a respectable status in north India. As the counter-balance to this, did the term *dāsa* come to be used for subordinated groups? *Dāsa*s associated with service occur but infrequently, and more so only a couple of times in the later sections (7.86.7; 1.92.8;

10.62.10). Ambiguities in the identities of the *āryas* and *dāsas* may have led to a gradual change in the connotation of both terms.

Dāsa and *dasyu* are used as nouns, but also gave rise to a verbal form, *abhidās*/to treat with hostility (1.79.11; 7.104.7). This would again question the use of *dāsa* in a racial or ethnic sense. References to physical differences are fewer and the majority of the adjectives refer to the absence of familiar ritual practices, linguistic abilities and generosity of patronage. Barring the single reference to *anāsa* (5.29.10), which has been read as either *a-nāsa*/noseless, or *an-ās*/without a mouth, i.e., language (5.29.10), and *vṛṣaśipra*/bull-jawed (7.99.4), and the uncertain meaning of *tvacam kṛṣṇām,* all of which have been the subject of much debate, it is the epithet *mṛdhra vāc* which is used frequently, as are the descriptions of the *dāsa* based on negative prefixes preceding what would be regarded as ideal qualities.

The many references to *mṛdhra vāc* are generally associated with *dasyu*s (7.6.3; 5.29.10; 5.32.8; 10.23.5; 1.74.2; 1.130.9; 7.18.9-13) and as noticed earlier, with the Pūrus. References in the late sections to the stealing of speech or to those speaking in a different way, emphasize the lack of familiarity of some with Indo-Aryan and yet the need for there to be social relations with such people (1.130.9; 10.23.5). Indra is said to humble the *mṛdhra vāc* which would not necessarily refer to the *dāsas* except that it continues with the statement that he breaks their autumnal *pur*s and gives them to Purukutsa, the Pūru chief (1.174.2). That the epithet *mṛdhra vāc* is used for a number of people makes it apparent that this was not the incorrect speech of a single person but was a reference to non-Indo-Aryan language speakers or to those using a faulty form of Indo-Aryan.

The significant differences between the *ārya*s and the *dāsa*s, apart from language, were that the *dāsa*s were seen as behaving in a contrary way to the *ārya*s, especially in matters relating to custom and ritual. They are described most often as *avrata*/

without laws or not observing the *vratas* (1.132.4; 1.175.3; 6.14.3; 1.33.5; 1.51.8; 1.130.8; 9.73.5-8), or as having other laws (9.41.2), as not performing the sacrificial ritual and particularly the *soma* rites (7.6.3), or having differences in ritual (1.33.4-9) or being without rites (10.22.8; 4.16.9). Their worship of the phallus/*śiśna-deva* is disapproved of (7.21.5) as also their indulgence in magic (8.14.14; 10.73.5-7). They are said to be foolish, niggardly, unfriendly (6.33.3), unthinking (10.22.8), greedy and avaricious (6.44.11; 5.7.10; 1.125.7), without generosity and stingy (1.84.8) and perhaps for this reason they demand ransoms and haggle (6.47.21).

The association with sorcery and magic recalls the presence of the *yātudhāna* elsewhere in the *Ṛgveda* and the frequency of their occurrence in the *Avesta* where the *yātu* is a demon or a wizard or sorcerer practising witchcraft and taking various forms[37] and is associated particularly with the Helmand/Haraxvaiti region of Afghanistan. The word has the same meaning in the *Ṛgveda* (7.104.23). The *yātudhāna* and the *rākṣasa* are mentioned together in some hymns which wish the destruction of both (7.104; 10.87; 10.118).

Above all the *dāsa*s are associated with wealth, *dhanin, rayim* (1.33.4; 8.40.1; 10.83.3). Their habitat is linked to the *pur*s which have to be rent asunder with the aid of the gods. This could suggest that they are sedentary unlike the *asuras* and the *rākṣasa*s. The *pur* could be any settlement generally with mud walls (7.6.5). These may have been nucleated villages containing habitations and cattle stockades or cow pens – *gotra*s – and whose closely knit layout both in the mountains of the borderlands and on the plains would have suggested a walled settlement, as the villages of these areas do to this day. The *gotra*/cow-pen, was not identical with the *pur* but may have been a part of it. A recent view maintains that the lay-out of the *pur* was concentric and parallels to this have been sought in structures at the site of Dashly-3 in north-eastern

Iran.[38] This would tend to revive the theory that some parts of the *Ṛgveda* may have referred to Afghanistan, an idea which has been re-iterated on other evidence as well.[39]

Wealth can be acquired through the destruction of the *pur*s (4.30.13) and where successful, the wealth was distributed (6.43.1- 4; 6.47.22-23). Again in the late sections of the *Ṛgveda* it is said that Indra destroys the *pur*s of the *adeva,* the godless (1.174.8) irrespective of who they are, whether they be *ārya* or *dāsa* (10.38.3). He is particularly effective after he has drunk *soma* (9.61.1-2). Sometimes the fantasy overtakes the reality. The cow stalls of the *dāsa*s replete with cattle are raided to obtain the animal herds. The killer of the *dasyu* goes stealthily towards the cow stalls and is in effect a cattle-raider (6.45.24). The association of horses with the wealth of the *dāsa*s would point to their location close to the Indo-Iranian borderlands from where the horses were obtained. Mention is also made of treasure, gold and garments (2.15.9; 3.34.9). The main wealth was in cattle and the words for cattle and cattle-related activities or as metaphors for these are the largest in number.

The refrain of the authors remains a prayer for wealth – *rayim dāḥ* – as almost a desperate appeal (10.47.1). Balbūtha and Tarukṣa, although *dāsa*s are respected because they were patrons, as was Bṛbu the *paṇi* (6.45.31-33). For them the authors of the hymns were willing to perform rituals in return for a handsome gift (8.46.32). Ritual becomes a mechanism of influence and communication. Clearly here the skin colour, whatever it may have been, did not intervene in accepting the patronage of those who were otherwise described as lawless and riteless.

Some *dāsa*s such as Śambara seem to be sneakingly admired. If Geldner's reading is correct then Indra changed from friendship to hostility towards Śambara. Thus the reference to him as a *dāsa* need not be because of a racial or ethnic origin but because of other reasons for hostility (6.47.14-21). A sign of Śambara's status was that both Indra and Agni on separate occasions are said to have struck him down (1.51.6; 1.59.6). In the reference to the *dāsas* Balbūtha and Tarukṣa there is a pointer to some assimilation where ritual plays a role. A gift of a hundred is said to have been given by the *dāsa* (8.46.32). Who was the recipient? Was he an *ārya* willing to accept a gift from a *dāsa* or was he perhaps of *dāsa* origin and had learnt the ritual of the *ārya* and was performing the sacrifice for a *dāsa* chief, but composing a *dāna-stuti* in the language of the *ārya*?

The readings of Sāyaṇa have been generally ignored in reconstructing the relations between the two. Although there is an enormous distance in time between the *Ṛgveda* and Sāyaṇa's commentary, and he obviously finds it as difficult to explain some passages as did Max Müller, Wilson, Griffith, Geldner and Renou and other modern scholars, nevertheless he tries to find explanations which are part of the "*itihāsa*", the perception of the past as it were, of the tradition. These may not be accurate from the perspective of linguistics but are of interest from the perspective of cultural history indicating the choice of explanation of a fourteenth century specialist on the *Veda*s. What is striking and contradicts modern interpretations is the absence of racial connotations in Sāyaṇa. Even if we cannot accept his explanations, this in itself is a very significant feature. What is even more striking is that Max Müller who included the commentary of Sāyaṇa in his edition of the *Ṛgveda*, seems to have seldom paused to question his own readings when they disagreed with Sāyaṇa.

IV

Various suggestions can be made in an attempt to explain the general relationship between *ārya* and *dāsa*. Claims to *ārya* status would initially have involved identities of language, ritual and custom and would have included those who had access to resources and power. The term may later have become generic, referring to groups claiming status, where the ethnic element was eroded and aryanisation took place through the adoption of the language, some significant rituals and beliefs, and the observance of particular social customs as later defined by the rules of *varṇa* as caste. Language would have been modified by the substratum speech of the areas where the Indo-Aryan speakers settled. Similar changes would have occurred in ritual. Such modifications are likely to have increased through single clan migrations and settlements. The shading off from *ārya* to *dāsa* became less distinctive and although the terminology was retained the membership of each of the initial two *varṇa*s would gradually change.

We can perhaps assume that the *ārya* observed the practices which are negated in the characteristics of the *dāsa*. The greed for *dāsa* wealth emphasized the duality in this relationship. The greed was articulated in the *dāna-stuti*s, in effect, hero lauds, although possibly the actual relations between *ārya, dāsa, paṇi,* and so on were based on more graduated differences. Three groups are involved: the authors of the hymns who are bards and ritual specialists and some of whom are seeking patronage, the *ārya*s who generally provide the patronage which it is said, is augmented by raiding the third group, that of the wealthy *dāsa*s. The hymns are prayers in which, apart from references to deities and rituals, are embedded the ballads of heroic exploits which give immortality to the heroes, and which also include appeals for wealth addressed to the generosity of the chiefs. A comparison of the language of the *Ṛgveda* with the later corpus has suggested that the language was incorporating elements of the Dravidian and Austro-Asiatic languages in the vicinity. Similar changes would doubtless occur in rituals and ways of life. The eventual working out of the *varṇa* statuses was in part an attempt at trying to control variance and stratification in societies especially where they involved dominance and subordination. It becomes more realistic if it is remembered that these mutations cover around five hundred years.

Conflicts over gaining wealth are reflected in the difference of language and social and ritual codes between those who have wealth and those who are seeking it. The wealth is largely pastoral and the pieces of gold could well have been an exaggeration as were the numbers of the animals. Status was dependent on birth into the clan claiming seniority, and had gradually but increasingly to be backed by wealth if the title of *rājan* had to be retained. Hence the continuing centrality of raids with the Kuru-Pañcālas a few centuries later raiding in the dewy season. Many of the hymns extol a desire for material wealth which is strangely discordant in a compilation of hymns addressed to deities. The title of *rājā/rājan* is not associated with the *dāsa*s nor are we told the names of their clans: this may be an indicator of treating them as of low status. Prayers to the gods are intended to ensure the killing of the enemy or to provide assistance in such destruction, the authors of the hymns not themselves indulging in the killing. The appropriation of enemy wealth is justified by maintaining that there was a moral righteousness in the conflict on the part of the authors. Because the *dāsa*s are without laws (as judged by the *ārya*s), without the correct rituals and language, they have to be subordinated and their wealth taken away from them. The enemies are invariably those who do not bestow wealth on the authors of the hymns as patrons. The hymns therefore reflect a potential discontent.

By the mid-first millennium the status of the *dāsa* takes on a different definition. He is no longer associated with large herds, arable land and wealth, but to the contrary, his identity is one that is devoid of these. If the meaning of *dāsa* was essentially 'the Other', then the wealthier *dāsa* patrons may have entered the ranks of the *ārya*s and the word *dāsa* eventually came to signify the impoverished 'Other', impoverished through the greed of the *ārya*s. If the *dāsa*s who held out against the *ārya* raids were the wealthy cattle-keepers, then once the raids had depleted their cattle resources, they would be impoverished.

Much of the activity in the *Ṛgveda* focuses on pastoralism but this does not imply an absence of agriculture, either as a complement to pastoralism or as an independent activity. Nor does it mean that pastoralists are to be regarded as somehow backward and primitive, for pastoralists had a variety of relationships with agriculturalists. Hero fights hero for cattle, water and arable land (2.21.2; 6.25.4; 10.50.3). Water was as necessary to a herd of animals as it was to irrigating fields. Fighting over fertile fields is mentioned (4.38.1; 6.20.1), but far less often than the capturing of cattle and pastures. The distinction between cultivable land and waste land is made in a late hymn which states that after Agni has burnt the brushwood, it resembles the waste land (or fallow land?) in between the cultivated (10.142.3).

Maintaining the size of the herd is crucial to pastoralism and the herd has to be reproduced, therefore raids for obtaining animals are frequent. Grazing grounds tend to be large and treated as assigned territory. Pitched battles tend to be rare although raids are frequent. Identity with territory becomes important to clans when they begin to be sedentary. The measuring of a field does not imply private property. Land is held by the clan even as late as in the *Brāhmaṇa*s,[40] and individual fields could be measured to calculate the distribution of agricultural produce. Possibly the centrality given to dicing and especially within the sanctity of the *sabhā* – the assembly hall – was not just for amusement but also for ascertaining by lot who had access to which pastures or fields – a practice known to some other societies.

Pastoralism and agriculture are interdependent activities nevertheless societies in this relationship of interdependence tend to favour one over the other. It would seem from the hymns of the *Ṛgveda* that the society of the *ārya*s was predominantly pastoral in the initial stages, gradually incorporating agriculture on a larger scale. Agriculture was part of the landscape and was a well-established activity among the existing populations. The plough goes back to pre-Harappan levels at Kalibangan.[41] Significantly, there appears to be a wider practice of agricultural activities among the speakers of Dravidian and Austro-Asiatic, judging from the borrowing of words from these languages for agricultural implements and processes by the authors of the *Ṛgveda*.[42] The *Śatapatha Brāhmaṇa* refers to the *asura*s as essentially cultivators.[43] The appropriation of cultivated land in two of the hymns appears to be associated with the Pūrus (4.38.1; 7.19.3-6) and as we have seen, the identity of the Pūrus is somewhat ambiguous.

The desire for wealth focuses on the capturing of cattle and moveable wealth rather than on ousting cultivators from arable land. A raiding relationship cannot be a long term relationship. Negotiations may have been a more effective way of relating to cultivators. This would be assisted by the symbiotic exchange of stubble for manure as also by the exchange of pastoral products for agricultural products. The grazing of animals on stubble provides manure for the fields. There is a striking infrequency of violence over fields as compared to raids for the capture of cattle. Mention is also made of fighting in the fields for cattle (5.33.4), or cattle wandering with a herdsman and eating the barley of the pious (10.27.8), which could perhaps be best understood as a reference to allowing cattle to graze on the stubble of the fields after the harvest.

This interdependence may have had other implications. Cultivation and the breeding of live stock continued to be practiced in the post-Harappan settlements, but these were now left without an overall political and administrative protection after the decline of the Harappan system. These would be times of intense insecurity and uncertainty, particularly if the *ārya*s fought each other as well as fighting the *dāsa*s. Did the villages therefore, eventually seek protection from the pastoral chiefs with whose clans there might already have existed a symbiotic relationship? The relationship could sometimes be based on mutual benefits and sometimes on pressures of a more coercive kind. The symbiosis would in any case have encouraged bilingualism. It is likely that it grew out of a juxtaposition in which the incoming pastoral chiefs would have had a dominant position underlined by their use of horses and chariots, and possibly in a later phase, some iron weaponry and this might in part account for the status of their language, Indo-Aryan. Protection, extended both to lesser kin groups as well as others seeking it, would help augment the wealth of the *rājan*s through the prestations and gifts from the *viś* thought to be voluntary at this stage and brought on ritual occasions, and which with repetition were to become more regular. Among the words from the non-Aryan languages inducted into Indo-Aryan a noticeable number relate to agriculture.

The introduction of Indo-Aryan coincided with various innovations but these may not have been sufficient for the establishing of a new language. Where social relationships were re-adjusted, involving old and new populations, there the emergence of dominant groups would ensure the preeminence of their language as well. And if the dominant group as pastoral chiefs spoke Indo-Aryan, this would after a while, emerge as the language of status.

Furthermore, if the *ārya* saw the *dāsa* as one without rites or without the proper rites, the performance of these rites would also become an avenue to better status. This would involve acknowledging the higher status of the ritual language and being familiar with it at a minimum level. Those *brāhmaṇa*s described as *dāsyāḥ-putra* would not only be familiar with it but claim expertise in it and would endorse its status. Ritual therefore, is also central to the differentiation. There is a moral righteousness in killing the *dāsa* because he is not performing the correct rites and therefore regarded as without rites/riteless. But when some *dāsa* chiefs become patrons of the correct rites and the ritual specialists accept *dāna* from them, then do these *dāsa*s become *ārya*s? An example of this might be the Pūrus. Similarly, were the rules of social custom such as those pertaining to marriage ignored when reference is made to the *brāhmaṇa*s, described as the sons of *dāsī*s, whose status is acknowledged in the *Brāhmaṇa*s.[44] They not only contravened social custom in their parentage but are likely to have introduced *dāsa* features into the ritual. Some may have been the ritual specialists of the existing societies perhaps included among the *yātudhāna*s of the *Ṛgveda*. Some may still have been conserving a few rituals from Harappan times. The two categories most likely to have survived from an earlier period would have been the ritual specialists and the providers of labour and prestations – and the two as always were interconnected. These social changes which are visible as traces in the *Ṛgveda* come to be established by the mid-first millennium when the *dāsa* is the impoverished 'Other', servile to the *ārya* and as a *śūdra* disallowed from performing the rituals of the *ārya*.

That Indo-Aryan contains non-Aryan elements reflects a growing social inter-face between various groups. The conflict between the categories of *ārya*s and of *dāsa*s seems to occur more frequently in the north-west. The *dāsa* as the enemy declines in the *Brāhmaṇas*, because of the internal social hierarchies which develop in this period. The mention of *dāsa* becomes less frequent and *dasyu* even less so, for it was being replaced by other categories of social distance and subordination, as for instance, the *śūdra*. A striking difference is that whereas the *dāsa* was excluded for not observing the rites of the *ārya,* but once he did so his patronage was accepted, the *śūdra* on the other hand was denied participation in these rites. The justification given for this exclusion and the ensuing subordination was the claim to ritual purity of what were to emerge as the upper castes and the degrees of pollution associated with those regarded as low. The exclusion was made permanent by associating it with being born into certain social categories. Even though the actual subordination resulted from changing requirements of labour and resources, the concept of ritual purity was made essential to social hierarchy. This brings about a new organization of these societies, where some existing categories were incorporated but the justification for inequality grew out of the new situation. Social and economic adjustments needed the sorting out of hierarchy.

V

The distinction between *ārya* and *dāsa* relates to language, ritual and social custom. Indo-Aryan evolved in the midst of other languages and even if it finally emerged as dominant, the influence of the other languages is evident. The social association of Indo-Aryan with the dominant groups such as the *rājan*s, possibly some of the *viś* and the ritual specialists, gradually established Indo-Aryan as the pre-eminent language. Those who spoke Indo-Aryan called themselves *ārya*s. The *rājan*s had access to resources such as horses and chariots and became the victorious cattle-raiders as well as protectors of those who sought protection. What also needs to be investigated is the kind of edge which new technology and knowledge might have given to those using Indo-Aryan.

In encapsulating social change the *Ṛgveda* is at one level concerned with externally differentiated societies, characterised by differences in languages, ritual and social laws. But the authorship of the hymns is restricted to only one of these – those that call themselves the *ārya*s. The maximum information is about the internal differentiations among the *ārya*s. The society of the *ārya*s was not an egalitarian society but had a hierarchy. The *rājan*s were the clan chiefs who led the raids and supervised the distribution of the booty. They were the ones to whom the *dāna-stuti* eulogies were addressed, whose status is reflected in epithets such as *sujāta*/the well-born one, and in attempts at scattered genealogical data. Subordinate to the *rājan* were the *viś* but who in some passages of the subsequent texts are said to have been close to the *rājan* in status. Were they both part of a lineage-based society where recruitment into the clan was by birth with the senior lineage having authority over the junior lineage, and status depended on rank and where relations of production, in a literal sense, were embedded in kinship?[45] This embedded relation gradually broke down when in the subsequent period the *viś* had to labour for the *rājan* and the voluntary *bali* took the form of a regular tribute. The category of *ṛtvij*/ritual specialist or *kavi*/bard, did not belong to the lineage but performed rites for the *rājan*s and composed eulogies on them. Mention is made of seven kinds of ritual specialists, including the *hotṛ*, *potṛ*, *neṣṭṛ*, *adhvaryu* and *brāhmaṇa* (2.1.2). However at this stage, there were some rituals which did not require that many specialists. The composition and compilation of the early sections of the *Ṛgveda* – what are referred to as the family books or *maṇḍala*s II to VIII – are by authors, some of whom were subsequently claimed as the eponymous ancestors of certain *brāhmaṇa gotras*. There would have been competition among them for the patronage of the chiefs.

Social and economic adjustments were a necessity in order to sort the internal hierarchy and to provide spaces for others to be slotted in. The later Vedic corpus and especially the *Brāhmaṇa*s show this process at work. There was a contestation between the established ritual specialist, the *brāhmaṇa* and the successor to the *rājan*, the powerful *kṣatriya*. The subordination of the *viś* to the *kṣatriya* came to be accepted. The significant change was the emergence of the *śudra* as non-kin labour, which category might have included the impoverished *dāsa*. This change would have further reduced the significance of the kin-embedded economy of earlier times.

Legitimation for these adjustments was sought in the theory of *varṇa* which was not a racial segregation but was the setting out of social categories, based on access to resources either directly as in the case of the *kṣatriya* or indirectly in the form of *dāna* and *dakṣiṇā* in the case of the *brāhmaṇa;* to authority and power, both temporal and through claims to association with deities; and to a distancing of those who provided labour through an insistence on their ritual impurity and therefore necessary exclusion. This has implications for the origins of *varṇa*. The enforcing of permanency was not only by insisting that status whether high or low was dependent on birth but by further introducing the theory of *karma* and *saṃsāra*, where rebirth was conditioned by observing the rules of *varṇa*.

Aryanisation, if one chooses to call it that, is not the victory of a racial group or the smooth imposition of one culture on another but the interface of many parameters. However it is not a neutral process. Those claiming to be *ārya*s must have proximity to political power and authority and to a control over resources; Indo-Aryan derived languages are expected to be the languages of high culture but may well incorporate elements of other languages which continue to be used; the divisions in society should follow the rules, in theory at least, of ritual status or *varṇa,* since the *ārya* is placed among the upper, twice-born castes; those viewed as powerless and having had to relinquish resources are subordinated and relegated to being providers of labour. This required control over social stratification, and the exclusion from rites and rituals of those who laboured, requirements which are re-iterated whenever such subordination becomes necessary. This historical process calls for further exploration.

Notes

1. I would like to thank Dr. K. Meenakshi, Professor F. Staal and Dr. Kumkum Roy for their comments on this paper and the subject which have helped me clarify some of my ideas.

2. Thapar R., 'The Theory of Aryan Race and India: History and Politics', *Social Scientist,* 1996, 24, 1–3, 3–29.

3. E.g. Gupta S. P., 'Longer Chronology of the Indus-Sarasvati Civilisation', *Puratattva,* 1992-93, 23, 21–29. Gupta S.P. (ed.), 1995, *The Lost Sarasvatī and the Indus Civilisation* (Jodhpur, Kusumanjali Publications). B. B. Lal had earlier identified the Aryans with the post-Harappan Painted Grey Ware culture and built his interpretation of archaeology and the epics on this. He now argues for the identity of the Harappan and Vedic cultures. Lal B. B., 'The Indo-Aryan Hypothesis viz-a-vis Indian Archaeology', *Journal of Central Asia,* 1978, 1.1.21ff.; Lal B. B., *The Earliest Civilisation of South Asia* New Delhi 1997, 281–7.

4. A number of studies reject this view and among them are Sharma R. S., *Advent of the Aryans in India,* Delhi 1997; R. Thapar et al., *India: Historical Beginnings and the Concept of the Aryan*, New Delhi 2006.

5. The tiger and the rhinoceros are reported from Sind and Punjab as late as in medieval sources.

6. Figures in brackets refer to the *maṇḍala,* the hymn and the verse, in the *Ṛgveda*. Where words are quoted from the text, the original grammatical form has been retained where required.

7. History and Culture of the Indian People, Vol. I, *The Vedic Age*, Bombay, 1956, 222ff.; 337 ff. Mallory J. P., *In Search of the Indo-Europeans*, London 1991. To argue that Indo-Aryan, Dravidian and Austro-Asiatic, all belong to the same linguistic family, as is stated by some enthusiasts supporting the indigenous origin of 'the Aryans', shows little understanding of linguistic structures and the clear differences of these in all three languages. For a start, Indo-Aryan is inflected whereas Dravidian is agglutinative.

8. Burrow T., 'The Proto-Indo-Aryans', *Journal of the Royal Asiatic Society,* 1973, 2, 123–40.

9. Parpola A., *Deciphering the Indus Script*, Cambridge 1994.

10. M.Witzel, 'Substrate Languages in Old Indo-Aryan (Ṛgvedic, Middle and Late Vedic)', *Electronic Journal of Vedic Studies,* 1999, 5,1,1–97.

11. Kuiper F. B. J., *Aryans in the ṚgVeda*, Amsterdam, Leiden Studies in Indo-European, No. I, 1991.

12. Thapar R., 'Exploring Societies of the Early Past', loc. cit. These were issues that I raised in my preliminary work on this subject in 1969 and later.

13. Hiebert F., 'South Asia from a Central Asian Perspective', in Erdosy G. (ed.), *The Indo-Aryans of Ancient South Asia: Language. Material Culture, Ethnicity*, Berlin 1995.

14. Trautmann T., *Aryans and British India*, Delhi 1997.

15. Allchin F. R. and B., *Origins of a Civilisation*, Delhi 1997.

16. Vendidad, Fargard 1.1. ff.

17. Witzel M., 'Rigvedic History: Poets, Chieftains and Polities', in Erdosy, op. cit., 307–56.

18. Vendidad, Fargard, 1.1.ff.; 2.9.ff.

19. Baudhāyana 18.44. Discussed in Witzel M, 'Rigvedic History: Poets, Chieftains and Polities', in Erdosy G. (ed.), *The Indo-Aryans of Ancient South Asia*, New Delhi 1997.

20. Gonda J., 'The Vedic Concept of *amhas'*, *Indo-Iranian Journal*, 1957, 1.33-60.

21. Dr. Meenakshi drew my attention to this.

22. Hale W. E., *Asura in Early Vedic Religion*, Delhi 1986.

23. Szemerenyi O., 'Studies in the Kinship Terminology of the Indo-European Languages', *Acta Iranica*, 1977, 7, 1–240.

24. Parallel to the changing concept of Aryan is the history of the concept of Bantu in Africa. See J. Vansina, 'New Linguistic Evidence and the Bantu Expansion', *Journal of African History*, 1995, 36, 173–95.

25. *Śatapatha Brāhmaṇa* 3.2.1.23. The *Brāhmaṇa*s were composed subsequent to the *Saṃhitā*s – such as that of the *Ṛgveda* – and were essentially an exegesis on the *Saṃhitā*s. They are generally dated to about 800 to 600 BC.

26. Thapar R., 'The Image of the Barbarian in Early India', *Ancient Indian Social History: Some Interpretations*, Delhi 1978, 152ff. Parasher A., *Mlecchas in Early India*, Delhi 1991.

27. 3.1.2.20.

28. Kuiper F. B. J., Review of R. Gordon Wasson, *Soma, Indo-Iranian Journal*, 1970, 12, 4, 179ff.

29. Renou L., *Études Vedique et Paninéenes,* XVII, 45, Paris 1955 sq.

30. Hock H., 'Subversion or Convergence?', *Studies in the Linguistic Sciences*, 1996, 23, 2, 73–115.

31. Geldner K. F., *Der Rig-Veda*, Cambridge, Mass. 1951.

32. Renou, op. cit. XVII, 35.

33. Vendidad, Fargard 8.80.

34. Thapar R., '*Dāna* and *Dakṣiṇā* as Forms of Exchange', *Ancient Indian Social History*, Delhi 1978, 105–121.

35. *Śatapatha Brāhmaṇa* 6.8.1.14.

36. *Śatapatha Brāhmaṇa* 3.2.3.15.

37. Vendidad, Fargard 8.80

38. Rau W., 'The Meaning of *Pur* in Vedic Literature', *Abhandlungen der Marburger Gelehrten Geselleschaft,* 1973, 1ff.; Parpola A., 'The Coming of the Aryans to Iran and India and the Cultural and Ethnic Identity of the Dāsas', *Studia Orientalia*, 1988, 64, 195–302.

39. Parpola, op. cit.; Witzel, op. cit.

40. *Śatapatha Brāhmaṇa* 13.7.1.15; *Aitareya Brāhmaṇa* 8.21.8.

41. Lal B. B., 'Perhaps the Earliest Ploughed Field so far Excavated Anywhere in the World', *Puratattva,* 1970-71, 4, 1ff.

42. Burrow T., *The Sanskrit Language*, London 1973 (3rd.ed.), 373 ff.; Kuiper, 1991, op.cit.

43. 1.6.1.4.

44. *Aitareya Brāhmaṇa* 2.19; *Kauśītaki Brāhmaṇa* 12.3.

45. Thapar R., *From Lineage to State*, Delhi 2000 (revised ed.), 21–69.

References

Bailey H. W., 'Iranian Arya and Daha', *TPS* 1959,71-115.

Burrow T., *The Sanskrit Language,* London 1973 (3rd ed.).

Geldner K. F., *Der Rig-Veda,* Cambridge Mass. 1951.

Gonda J., 'The Vedic Concept of *Amhas' IIJ, 1957,* 1. 33–60.

Griffith R. T. H., *Hymns of the Rigveda,* Varanasi 1963 (reprint).

Hock H., 'Subversions or Convergence?', *Studies in the Linguistic Sciences,* 1996, 23, 2, 73–115.

Kuiper F. B. J., Review of R. Gordon Wasson, *Soma, IIJ,* 1970, 12.4.179ff.

Kuiper F. B. J., *Aryans in the Rigveda,* Amsterdam 1991.

Max Müller F., *Rig-Veda Samhita,* Varanasi 1983 (reprint).

Parasher A., *Mlecchas in Early India,* Delhi 1991.

Parpola A., 'The Coming of the Aryans to Iran and India', *Studia Orientalia,* 64, 1988, 195–302.

Rau W., 'The Meaning of *Pur* in Vedic literature', *AMGG*, 1973.1. Munich.

Renou L., *Études Vediques et Paninéenes,* I–XVII, Paris 1955 sq.

Thapar R., '*Dāna* and *Dakṣiṇā* as Forms of Exchange', *Indica* 1976, reprinted in *Cultural Pasts*, Delhi 2000.

Thieme P., *Der Fremdling im Rgveda,* Heidelberg 1938.

Trautmann T., *Aryans and British India,* Delhi 1997.

Witzel M., 'Rgvedic History: poets, chieftains and politics', in G. Erdosy, (ed.), *The Indo-Aryans of Ancient South Asia,* Berlin, 1995, 307–352.

5.

The Archaeological Background to the *Agnicayana* Ritual

For many decades now scholars have been waiting expectantly for archaeology to reveal a culture that can be definitively labelled as 'Aryan', but the Aryans remain elusive. It is likely that they will continue to remain so until a new definition of the term Aryan can be suggested. Such a clarification would not be entirely out of the question, considering that we are still working with a definition that derives essentially from concepts prevalent during the nineteenth century. Now that there is a fuller picture of the succession of archaeological cultures in northern India for the period with which the emergence of an Aryan culture can be associated, the continuing absence of a clearly identifiable Aryan culture may suggest that Aryanism is not an isolated, uniform culture but a system that draws on a multiplicity of cultures that remain crucial to the manifold forms it takes in time and space. In such a system, some facets of what have been called Aryan culture may find correlates in archaeological artefacts and assemblages, and these correlates may help us to redefine the culture. The purpose of this essay is to consider whether the description of the *agnicayana* in the Vedic corpus is reflected in the archaeological remains of the proto-historic period.

An *agnicayana* ritual was performed in Kerala in 1975. Those of us who were present as observers were able to reflect further on the co-relation between textual description and its possible material counterpart. Two problems became immediately apparent. Each source of evidence because of its different chronology has a different way of absorbing change in the course of evolving. A comparison requires examining the actual process of making an object. This I have tried to do for a few objects that occur in both sources. The other problem is one that crops up frequently in the use of ritual objects. In the making of some kinds of ritual objects a deliberately archaic technique is used, both to suggest antiquity as well as to differentiate the ritual object from similar objects in mundane use. This appears to be so in the making of the pottery used in the *agnicayana* ritual. Some degree of technical expertise is therefore necessary when comparing objects from textual and archaeological sources.

The attempt to identify the Aryan-speakers with archaeological remains is perhaps a pointless exercise. The Aryans were not a distinct racial group with a recognizable assemblage of material culture carefully carried across mountain and desert in the process of migration. Perhaps the most tangible characteristic of their presence was their language which was being diffused. This would not necessarily have required a chain of artefacts belonging to a uniform culture. Nor would language diffusion necessarily be registered in a uniform material culture. This is apparent from the presence of languages derived from Indo-European in Iran and Afghanistan, a development that is recognized not by an identical ceramic or artifactual industry but by the introduction of Indo-European languages.

At a hypothetical level a possible reconstruction could be suggested. The earliest Aryan speakers, as pastoralists, could have moved across the Indo-Iranian borders, settling temporarily in the interstices of cities. If the movement across the borders was regular, they might have provided transportation for small items of trade, as is often the case with pastoral groups involved in either transhumance or seasonal migrations.[1] Possibly small settlements evolved over time and maintained relations with the existing population in the second millennium BC.[2] That the main period of settlement came after the decline of the Harappan cities would seem likely from the absence of descriptions of cities in the *Ṛgveda*. The occasional references to the destruction of the *pur*s could as well refer to the walled settlements of the borderlands. The decline of the Harappan urban centres would have reduced the incentive to pastoral groups as carriers of trading items. This may have encouraged a more permanent type of settlement with seasonal camps turning to agriculture, and the settlements may well have extended to the 'two grassy banks of the Sarasvatī', as the hymns of the *Ṛgveda* state.[3] Iran was proximate to the Assyrian political system, therefore cultural divergence would be natural. Assyrian sources refer to Indo-European speakers in the Zagros area by the early first millennium BC.[4] Were the Asuras, who were once friendly and then became the enemies, the worshippers of either Asura or of Ahura? Such settlements would initially make little impact on the existing culture apart from marginal changes with the introduction of new items brought from elsewhere. Their archaeological identification would be equally difficult. (If the West Asian evidence is a fair parallel, then we can posit that agro-pastoral groups would tend to appropriate the material culture of the more settled agrarian communities). Textual evidence for the appearance of nomads in West Asia generally takes the form of the introduction of new names, the use of a different language, and the intrusion of new deities.[5]

Their survival would hinge on the maintenance of their own language and oral tradition. Linguistic purity can be maintained in an oral tradition up to a point, but the influence of the bilingualism accompanying a pastoral circuit would also come to be reflected in certain linguistic changes. In the juxtaposition of Aryan-speakers with descendents of earlier cultures, there could be either the conquest of the existing population, for which the archaeological evidence is limited, or else the assertion of power by the Aryan-speakers over the settled population, through a mutual acculturation resulting in new cultural forms and the acceptance of the Aryan language. It is legitimate to ask how the language came to be accepted if there is such negligible evidence for invasion. One possibility may have been the simultaneous appropriation of iron technology, together with such innovations as the central function of the horse[6] and the chariot, which may have acted as technological levers to give an edge to the culture of the Aryan speakers. The spread of the language would in any case have been a gradual process. This admixture of cultures and languages is perhaps what is reflected in the later Vedic texts and their possible archaeological correlations.

The *Ṛgveda* would then represent the erstwhile migratory pastoralists now settled, still largely clan-based holding cattle as their main wealth, practicing religious rites with a component of shamanism, alienated from some indigenous groups but affiliated with others, and possibly appropriating into their tradition some of the past of the land where they had settled. The first millennium BC saw a movement southwards and eastwards from the watershed attributable to ecological changes, to interaction with existing cultures, and possibly to demographic and economic pressure that favoured settling in new lands. Archaeological interactions are perhaps reflected in the distribution of the Painted Grey Ware and the Black-and-Red Ware cultures.

The form that Vedic culture took in the first millennium BC, the period of the descriptions of rituals such as the *agnicayana*, would seem to be an amalgam of existing cultures. Possibly the comprehension of ritual and symbol was blurred as much by the distance in generations from the earliest practice of these rituals as by the incorporation of originally alien systems. The ritual of the *agnicayana* would then have to be seen as symbolizing this amalgam of cultures, going back to the shamanism of Indo-European days, the sacrificial cult of Ṛgvedic practice, forms of possible Harappan survivals, and the accretion of more recent practices, perhaps taken from the Black-and-Red Ware cultures. That there is an elaboration of some significance between the rituals as described in the *Ṛgveda* and the same rituals as described later in the other Vedic texts is apparent if a comparison is made of references to the *aśvamedha*, for example. The *Ṛgveda*[7] describes a relatively simple ritual in which the horse is sacrificed for the acquisition of wealth, prosperity, and magical power. In the later texts it becomes an elaborate ritual incorporating the fire altar and consisting of many levels of activities spread over many months.[8] The ceremonies come to include fertility rites and the notion of a potlatch. The latter is as much a declaration of political ascendency and social status as the sending forth of the horse, and this becomes even more evident in the descriptions of the *aśvamedha* in the *Mahābhārata*[9] and the *Rāmāyaṇa*.[10] The *yajña*, sacrificial ritual, would represent the coming together of many rituals of diverse origins.

The search for the remnants of the *agnicayana* ritual in archaeological data is made more difficult by the fact that the structures associated with the ritual – sheds with thatched roofs supported by wooden posts – are made of perishable materials. The only exception is the altar, which was built of bricks. Was this done because the initial ritual was connected with migratory groups? Or because it did not require permanent sacred centres? Or was it done deliberately so that the area demarcated as sacred space could be desanctified at the termination of the ritual to leave only the altar? Equally striking is the fact that the objects used are primarily of clay and wood, so there is an absence of utility metals such as copper or iron. Yet copper, at least – and to a lesser extent iron – was familiar to first millennium people. The offerings of ghee, curd, milk, grain, *soma*, and domesticated animals would have been available to pastoralists and agriculturalists.

That the building and worship of fire altars may have gone back to the Harappan period remains a hypothetical suggestion. Brick altars have not been found in association with Harappan sites, nor are they represented symbolically on the Harappan seals. It has been suggested, however, that fire altars may have been known to the Harappans, or more correctly to those living in Lothal and in Kalibangan.[11] At Lothal a few small rectangular structures have been called fire-altars. In Kalibangan some tub-shaped earthenware structures were found inside the houses in the residential area as well as on a platform of the citadel area. In the latter case they were placed five in a row near a well, but a cut had been made through them at some later period by the construction of a brick-lined drain. The structures were approximately three to four feet in length and about half that in width. In the center of each was an upright stone cylinder with a series of terracotta cakes arranged around it. Traces of ash were visible on the inner side of the structure. These structures are clearly very different in concept and form from the Vedic even if it is assumed that they were fire altars. They could have been hearths. The resemblance would at best be symbolic, and even then rather farfetched. The closest to possible fire-altars are at Mehrgarh. It is also curious that these structures should be found only at a couple of Harappan sites. At most it can be argued that some rudimentary ritual connected with fire altars was known at this early period, and that this may have survived in altered garb when incorporated into the highly complex ritual connected with the *agnicayana*.

Many decades ago a seminal idea was mooted by Caland in a comment on an excavation by Bloch of a mound at Lauriya Nandangarh,[12] a site better known for an Aśokan pillar located in the vicinity. The site contained three rows of five mounds between twenty and fifty feet high. They were cone-shaped but may originally have been hemispherical. The mound was built up of layers of yellow clay interspersed with layers consisting of straw, leaves, and burnt bricks made from the same clay. Since this was not local clay, it was specially brought, probably from the Gandak river, which is now at a distance of about ten miles from the site. The first mound revealed human bones, animal bones, burnt wood, and a gold plaque of a female figure. A large opening farther down and in the center appears to have held a wooden pillar; the stump of the pillar on excavation was found to be of sal wood and to have a girth of four feet four inches. The second mound contained animal bones. The third contained human bones, the jaw of a teenaged child, and another golden plaque of a female figure.

Bloch thought these mounds to be the *śmaśāna*s or burial places referred to in the Vedic texts, possibly royal burials, but Caland argued that *śmaśāna*s are generally not round.[13] More pertinently, Caland questioned the placing of animal bones and the plaques of females in the human funeral mound. He suggested that these might instead have been *agnicayana* altars, arguing that according to the texts they could have been of various shapes – hawk-shaped, square, round, and so on. They were to be built in five layers interspersed with sand. In the lowest layer was placed the golden form of a man symbolising Puruṣa or Prajāpati, who is sometimes depicted with milk-giving breasts.[14] (In the case of the Nandangarh plaques however, the female genitalia are unmistakable.) In this layer were also to be placed the head of a man, a ram, a goat, a bull, and a horse; they could either be natural or made of clay. He was puzzled, however, by the wooden post in the center of the mound.

Kane has drawn attention to the statement that those who had performed the *agnicayana* were permitted a structure of bricks or clods at burial, suggesting an association of ideas if not a clear link between the *śmaśāna* and the *agnicayana*.[15] This in turn suggests a link between the terms *citi* and *caitya*.[16] *Caitya*, a form of *cetiya*, is ultimately derived from *citi*, the etymology of which refers to the act of 'heaping up.' A *citi* is a structure that results from a piling up of material in a particular form. Where the piling up was of bricks, the form would be more precise, and where it was of earth or clods of earth, the tumulus and the cairn would be 'natural' in form. The *cetiya* would then be either a sacred enclosure marking a sacred spot or, when it contained the relics of those who had died, a sepulchral monument. Buddhist literature refers to it in both these senses.[17] Paul Mus has suggested that the Vedic altar was the starting point of what developed into the Buddhist *caitya* and *stūpa*.[18] Presumably the *yūpa* associated with the altar may have become the central pivot in the raising of a tumulus. A distinction is made between the *śmaśāna*, which is essentially a funerary marker, and the *caitya*, which is a sacred enclosure. In the latter capacity the site could presumably be of a sacrifice or ritual, or even of an object of worship that had been cordoned off, such as the *aśvattha* tree. The earliest reference to a *caitya* appears to be in the *Āśvalāyana Gṛhyasūtra*.[19] The epics also indicate familiarity with the worship of *caitya*s in various forms.[20] In the *Rāmāyaṇa* *caitya*s are mentioned more frequently in connection with the *rākṣasa*s. Hanumān takes great pride in destroying the tall *caitya-prāsāda* in Lanka and uprooting its massive pillar.[21] That this was not regarded as an act of desecration would suggest that *caitya*s were perhaps linked with heterodoxy by this time.

Because of the etymological link between the words, it is assumed that the *cetiya* is a later form of the *citi*. It is possible, however, that the two, the Vedic altar and the tumulus, were parallel forms indicating places requiring veneration, and that the difference in form related to differences in the cults and rituals followed by various social groups. The *stūpa* becomes a more elaborate form of the tumulus with a variety of symbolic embellishments. It is curious that in the listing of forms which the *citi* can take, mention is made of the *rathacakra* and the *samūhya* or *dhānyarāśi*,[22] which occur in *stūpa* construction respectively as the spoked-wheel foundation and the paddy-heap shape.

Such burial mounds are generally dated to the first millennium BC on the basis of archaeological evidence and references in both Vedic and Buddhist literature. The worship of *caitya*s and *stūpa*s is regarded as customary even before the rise of Buddhism. Although *stūpa* architecture was made more elaborate in the Mauryan period[23] and later, the structure existed earlier, as shown for example in the record of Aśoka Maurya visiting and enlarging the Konakamana *stūpa*.[24]

It is significant that there is no mention of the *citi* as an altar of bricks in the *Ṛgveda*.[25] The development of the idea therefore may date to the period of the later texts, which represent the assimilation of Aryan and non-Aryan practices. In this connection[26] it has been pointed out that the burial practices of the Asuras, Prācyas (easterners), and others described in the *Śatapatha Brāhmaṇa* bear a close resemblance to the Megalithic remains from the Jungal Mahal area, that is, to the Vindhyan outliers in the districts of Banda, Mirzapur, and Varanasi. The monuments are basically cairn circles and cist circles constructed of stone, and the dominant feature is the piling up of stones into a cairn. There is, however, no use of bricks anywhere presumably because stone was easily available. The cairns enclose a pit that in most cases contains some human bones indicating postcremation burial and some animal bones associated with ritual killing, and there is one in which the bones of a tortoise and a rodent were found. The pottery is of various kinds ranging from an ill-fired red ware to the technically more sophisticated Black-and-Red Ware. These monuments date to the first half of the first millennium BC. Megalithic monuments serve the function in some cases of memorial monuments,[27] and in others of funerary monuments, a combination that appears to be reflected in the *caitya*s of a later period. From both points of view these Megalithic monuments would be regarded as sacred enclosures. There may possibly have been some connections with these monuments in the fashioning of the forms and the symbolism of the *agnicayana*.

By the first millennium BC there appears to have been a bifurcation in the rituals relating to death. The Harappans and most of the post-Harappan Chalcolithic cultures buried the dead with a predominance of urn burials or graves of various kinds. The Painted Grey Ware culture registers a noticeable absence of burials, suggesting that possibly cremation was the more regular form and was also legitimized in the Vedic texts. Given the social stratification that had emerged by this time, graves would almost certainly have been linked to persons or families of high status. However, the bifurcation is cultural and ethnic rather than social, since the Asuras and others are generally said to have had graves and burial mounds. The burial of the golden man, identified at some points with Prajāpati, who then passes to the invisible world of immortality to become the symbol of the immortal self and of the attainment of immortality by the *yajamāna*, indicates that burial rites may be woven into the *agnicayana*. The fact of the altar being a fire altar obliquely introduces the notion of cremation. The extent to which the *agnicayana* uses both burial and fire as symbols was perhaps a concession on the part of those who cremated the dead to the alien but older ritual of burial.

The *agnicayana* altar, as it is most frequently described, was a large construction of brick requiring a substantial output in time and energy and a fair knowledge of geometry, since the bricks are of prescribed shapes and sizes.[28] The unit is a square, one-fifth of the height of the sacrificer, and hence called the *pañcami* brick. Another tradition states that it should be one-fourth of the length of the *yajamāna*. Other shapes are variations on this, the basic measurement being sub-units of one-half, one-fourth, and one-eighth. A large-sized brick, the *adhyardha*, is rectangular in shape with the longer side measuring one and one-half times that of the *pañcama* and the short side equal to that of the *pañcama*, which in turn is subdivided to accommodate the long and the short quarter. The *sapāda* brick is again rectangular, with the long side being one and one-quarter the length of the *pañcama*. Subdivision of the squares and the rectangles results in triangular bricks of various shapes, which are particularly handy in shaping the pointed contours of a hawk altar. The thickness of the brick is described as being one-fifth of the distance between the *yajamāna*'s knees and the ground. This measurement is ambiguous, since the ratio of this distance to the full length of the *yajamāna* is not given.

Hyla Converse has drawn attention to the fact that brickmaking was a Harappan activity, and the details given for the making, shaping, and firing of these bricks may have derived from Harappan survivals.[29] The ratios of sizes of bricks from pre-Harappan and Harappan levels tends to be 1:2:3 and 1:2:4 in terms of thickness, breadth, and length. The size of the brick for the fire altar, i.e., 1:1 or 1:1.5, is also known from protohistoric sites, but it is not common. Since the ratio of the thickness of the brick to its breadth and length is of uncertain measurement, if the first ratio is deleted, then the size of the pre-Harappan brick would conform to 1:1.5, the size of the *adhyardha*. The sheer number of the bricks is also of some consideration. Most texts agree that the number should be 1000, with 200 bricks going into each of the five layers; but some texts mention the figure of 10,800.[30] The size of the brick as defined by one-fifth of the length of the *yajamāna* would under any circumstances be large. Such an effort would require the labor of a settled population over some months and is unlikely to have been easily carried out by groups of migratory pastoralists. This might in part explain why fire altars of packed earth are permitted in some texts, although the *Yajurveda* requires it to be built of brick.[31]

Among the other objects that suggest some echo of Harappan affiliation are the discoid wheels of the carts. These consisted of the *śakaṭa*, the large cart for transporting the *soma* in the ritual, and the *ratha*, the small cart used for oblations. The Harappans, it is thought, were unfamiliar with the spoked wheel. This is first mentioned in the *Ṛgveda*.[32] Toy carts in terracotta from Harappan sites have disc wheels.

Among the most obvious of the material objects that can be compared with archaeological remains is the pottery used in the ritual. The pottery vessels required in the *agnicayana* ceremony are the *ukhā*, in which the fire is deposited and maintained for many months;[33] the *mahāvīra*, which is used in the *Pravargya* rite associated with the *soma* sacrifice; and a few other pots used in the ritual.[34]

The making of these pots is described in detail in the texts. The clay has to be mixed with a large number of other things – varieties of earth, pieces of animal hair, plants, fragments of potsherds from deserted places (*armayāni kapālām*), and powdered pebbles. In the case of the *ukhā*, the water used for moistening the clay has to be boiled with the resin of the *palāśa* tree, and the ingredients mixed into the clay include iron rust. The technique suggested is that of coiling and dabbing to produce the actual shape of the pots. In one text this is to be done by a skilled potter, but in most other texts it is done by the *yajamāna* or his wife, or by members of the three *dvija* castes. The potter's wheel is known but is prohibited. The same clay mixture was to be used for making certain other pots, such as those used for milking, the vessel for ghee, and the disc-like potsherds for keeping certain offerings. The pots were first to be sun-dried, then 'plastered over' (perhaps the application of a slip). The *mahāvīra* has to be smoothed by using *gavedhuka* grass. The pots are then well fumigated (*dhūpayati*) with dried horse dung before being fired (*pacati*) in a pit or open-hearth kiln, where they are to be placed in an inverted position.[35] In the description given for the firing of the *ukhā*, a four-cornered pit is dug in which fuel is laid. On it are placed some of the bricks and the *ukhā*, the latter in an inverted position. Above this comes another layer of fuel. The fuel is then kindled for the firing, which lasts the length of the day, and the fuel is replenished when required. If any of the pots crack in the process, they should be repaired, and if they break, then new ones are to be made to replace them. Preparations for the making of some of the bricks were to take place at the same time as the making of the pots.

The *mahāvīra* should be one span high with a broad base and narrowed in the middle.[36] Another text describes it as being the shape of a wooden cup with either three or five elevations.[38] The top of the cup seems to have had a spout that would facilitate pouring. The *ukhā* should be one span high and a little more than a span in width, with a girdle around it and vertical strips.[38] The girdle is decorated with two to eight udders (breasts) with nipples. This would suggest an open-rimmed, oval pot. The pots used for milking are described as having the shape of the lip of the elephant, with a beak-like form for pouring similar to a ladle without a handle.[39] None of these shapes occur in Harappan pottery.

The potter and the potter's wheel are known both from the literary and the archaeological sources of this period. The insistence that the pots be hand-made may have been an attempt to distinguish ritual pottery from that for daily use; this could be to remove ritual pottery from the pollution of the potter and the potter's wheel, assuming of course that the potter's status was already low, and perhaps also to invest ritual pottery with an ancient association by debarring the use of the wheel. The injunction against the use of the potter's wheel is stated in one text with reference to the making of the milking pots.[40] The fact that such specific directions are given for the making of these pots may suggest that there might also have been a functional reason for using this technique.

The admixture of material to the clay would have produced a coarse-grained pottery more akin to early Neolithic handmade pottery than the finely levigated ceramics of the Chalcolithic period. The purpose of the mixture is explained in ritualistic terms, and various deities are invoked, which suggests shamanistic survivals. Technically, the use of what modern potters call 'grog' as a filler, which produces a clay mixed with crushed potsherds and small particles of pebbles, results in a mixture that is difficult to throw on a wheel because of the meagerness of levigated clay; it is more likely to be successful if the pot is handmade. Wheel-thrown pots require well-levigated clay, the finer the better. The advantage of using grog is that such pottery is less likely to crack when it comes into direct contact with fire. Thus, for the purposes for which the *ukhā* was made, i.e., to be used as a fire pan, a mixture with the clay would be essential. That the same technique was extended to other pots used in the ritual would suggest that there was some attempt at archaicizing the process.

The use of grog would also ensure less shrinkage at the green-hard stage when the pot is dried before firing.[41] The inclusion of hair, which would burn up in firing, served the same function. Iron rust may have acted as a fluxing agent to prevent the pot from collapsing when fired. Water boiled in resin may have assisted in providing an adhesive texture. The fumigation of pots before firing is a recognized technique in making primitive handmade black pottery; it fills in the pores with the soot particles that darken the pot.[42] Such pottery is generally fired below sinter point, often because the use of a crude kiln does not permit a high enough temperature and results in a porous fabric. Grog was probably also necessary because the firing was done in a pit rather than a regularly built kiln, with no separator between the actual pot and the fire, unless the layer of bricks fired with the pots acted as a separator. In any case, an open-hearth kiln can only fire to low temperatures, and the clay would have to be porous to prevent cracking.

The archaeological correlations of this pottery remain enigmatic. Neolithic potting techniques would go back to the fourth millennium BC in the Indo-Iranian borderlands and to the third millennium in the Deccan. But clearly the potter's wheel and more advanced techniques of kiln firing were also known in north India; therefore the technique for making pots other than the *ukhā* seems to have been deliberately archaic. There are no clear parallels to the shapes described, merely some suggestive similarities. There is one pottery form, referred to as having been found at Dabar Kot in the Loralai area, that is described as a cup with a channel spout,[43] and it does suggest a beak-like spout resembling the lip of an elephant! Pottery with udderlike elevations is rare in the ceramic assemblage of protohistoric India. A reference has been made to such a find at a site on the bank of the Tungabhadra at Itgi in Belgaum district, where a black oval pot was found with the required nipple-like decoration and with the prescribed two holes in the base through which a cord could be passed to enable the *yajamāna* to carry the pot.[44] However, the excavator dates this pot to the first century BC or AD, not contemporary with the texts but with a later ritual event.

The statement in the texts that the pots have to be placed in an inverted position for firing in the pit kiln has been interpreted as a possible reference to the inverted firing technique common to the widespread pottery of the Black-and-Red Ware culture.[45] But if the intention was to produce a double colour, then it is likely that the texts would have referred to this as a mark of distinction of the ritual pottery. Hyla Converse has argued that this was perhaps the secret technique that receives an ambiguous mention in the text. Reference to the colour of the pottery is limited to one text that stipulates that the pots be fired to a red colour.[46] To produce a black-and-red colour would require controlled firing. Dry fuel and a good draft produce the oxidizing atmosphere necessary to make red pottery, whereas damp fuel and an obstructed draft are required to prevent oxidation and provide the reducing atmosphere necessary to make black pottery. A pit kiln such as the one described would have resulted in an indiscriminate mixture. The inversion of the pot may have had to do with ease of placing the pot in the pit. Pots are often placed in an inverted position in an open-hearth kiln, and the black and red tones that result can be accidental. The depth of the open-hearth kiln would also be significant. A deep pit would obstruct the flow of air. The reference in the texts to the bamboo handle of the spade disappearing in the pit would indicate a deep pit. In the description given for the making of the *mahāvīra*, there seems to be less admixture of grog, perhaps because unlike the *ukhā* this pot was not used for carrying fire. The *mahāvīra* is smoothed, perhaps to facilitate its handling. Curiously no reference is made to digging a pit when the pot is fired in an open-hearth kiln. This may be assumed, but it is worth noting that a shallow pit or a surface-level hearth would encourage a freer flow of air than a deep pit, thus permitting oxidation and resulting in a red-colored pottery. One text states specifically that the fuel to be used, including dry herbs, wood, etc., should be such as would produce a red-coloured pottery.[47]

If the reference to inverted firing had to do with the Black-and-Red Ware culture, then it poses another problem. A reference to *nīla-lohita* in the *Atharvaveda*[48] is taken by some scholars to refer to the Black-and-Red pottery. If this be so, then the text disapproves of the practices of those who use this pottery, giving it an Asura connection. This is also hinted at in the statement that the *ukhā* is born of the *asuri māyā*.[49] The *Ṛgveda* links some Asuras with the Angirasas, who are believed to be the priests of the fire cult.[50]

To add further complications, the texts also speak of the 'smoothing' of the pots. It has been assumed that the outer surface of the pottery was black, and that therefore the reference to the polishing of this pottery may hint at a relationship with the Northern Black Polished Ware of the mid-first millennium BC.[51] The latter is late on the ceramic scene, has its provenance in the middle Ganga valley, and was made possible through development of a highly evolved technique of firing at temperatures, that, it has been suggested, were probably attainable only after the invention of iron smelting. The nomenclature is deceptive, since the polish is not due to any post-firing technique but probably results accidentally through the interaction of natural constituents of the clay, or the addition of some special ingredient. It is generally associated with the luxury ware of the urban centres in the pre-Mauryan and Mauryan periods. In fact, the method for polishing pots described in the texts could more correctly be interpreted as a form of burnishing, a method used for the smoothing of the exterior surface of handmade pottery and already a common practice in the making of Neolithic pottery. This is further supported by the fact that the burnishing of pottery is usually done at the green-hard stage prior to firing, and polishing is a post-firing technique. The texts are clear that the 'smoothing' is to be done prior to firing. The purpose of burnishing was literally to smooth the exterior surface, but it was also employed to make the pot less porous or to add a decorative feature.

In the ceremonial space used for the performance of the *agnicayana*, there is only one structure that is likely to survive, namely the altar. Consequently, the presence of an altar is the only major clue to the site of an actual performance of the ritual. Claims to have identified such sites from archaeological remains are extremely few, and of these only one is accepted as genuine, since it carries an inscription describing it as an altar. This extreme paucity of evidence may have to do with the fact that such altars are required to be constructed on ground that has been sanctified and demarcated, and that therefore is likely to be at some small distance from settlements. Archaeological excavation is primarily of settlements, and it is largely by chance that such an altar may be found in the process of exploration.

Controversy still swirls around the identification of a *śyenaciti* on the outskirts of the ancient city of Kauśāmbi dating to the mid-first millennium BC.[52] The *śyenaciti* is located on the outside of the eastern gate, but close to the defence wall of the city, and it is bounded by the revetment of the rampart and its returning wall. The altar, in the shape of a bird (eagle?) with outstretched wings, faces southeast. It has a length of 49 feet 8 inches and a width of 33 feet 6 inches. In the construction of the altar the first layer of bricks was sealed by a sand deposit of 6 inches. In its center was a gravel (*kaṅkara*) nodule – with small cavities enclosed by a circle of 10 bricks – that the excavator takes to be the *svayamātṛṇa*. The most noticeable pottery object was shaped like an offering stand with a broken top approximately 5 inches high. In the same layer was included a terracotta female figurine, stylistically datable to about the second or first century BC. The excavator also describes a brick with an engraving of a man tied to a stake who is about to be beheaded. There is a scatter of animal bones – a horse skull, tortoise shell, the jawbone of a pig, and the bones of elephants, bovines, and goats, the last three having been verified as such. Also included in this layer was an iron model of a snake. Layer II seals off the jawbone of a buffalo and bricks of various shapes. Layer III produced three complete human skulls and some skull fragments, and also hipbones, ribs, and long bones. Some bones bearing incision marks were arranged in a V-shape or were enclosed in brick structures suggesting careful placement and some ritual function. Layers IV and V were badly damaged by a pit from a later period that had been dug into these layers, but they nevertheless provided evidence of human bone fragments. There were also a human skull and some pots placed in the tail section of the altar.

The identification of the site as a fire altar does raise some problems. The location of the altar so close to the ramparts of the city seems unusual. Given the fact that the altar is part of a ritual that requires the demarcation of sacred space, it seems strange that it should not have been placed farther from the city wall. The excavator quotes a reference in the *Kandahāla Jātaka* to a king digging a sacrificial pit just outside the eastern gate of the city.[53] It could be argued that the site was away from the original wall of the city but that the later extension of defences and the building of revetments resulted in encroachment on the altar space. This would depend on the date of the altar. If the terracotta figurine is not a stray from a later period, then the altar may well date to a period subsequent to the reinforcing of the city walls. The shape of the bird as presently reconstructed appears to be rather curvilinear, whereas the bricks used for the altar would indicate a more rectilinear form. The interpretation of the objects found is also not convincing.[54] The engraving on the brick of a man tied to a stake would seem to appear to be such only in the eyes of the excavator, if one can judge by the photograph; nor is the iron model of the snake recognizable. The pottery object described as an offering stand bears greater resemblance to a wide-mouthed jar. The frequency of human skulls and bones would also seem to suggest a ritual different from that described in the texts and it certainly is in excess of what is required. The texts refer to the burial of the head of a man, ram, goat, bull, and horse. The skulls of all but the human are absent in this *śyenaciti*, although their bones are there.

Whether or not the *śyenaciti* is in strict conformity with the descriptions of the fire altar in the literary sources, and whether or not the interpretation of objects as given by the excavator is acceptable, there can be little doubt that the structure did represent some kind of sacrificial or funerary site. The brick structure was built to some specification. The large number of human bones and the associated animal bones would point to a ritual connection. If the site is as late as the first century BC, then it is possible that some pragmatic changes were introduced into the rituals described in the texts. The site was evidently disturbed in later periods, and this may have been accidental, although the possibility that such sites were believed to contain treasure may account for many tumuli having been broken into.

Another place with far less evidence was also rumored to have provided an altar site. This was the town of Nagarjunakonda in the Paland taluka of Guntoor District. The inscriptions of the Ikṣvāku kings who ruled here in the second and third centuries AD refer to the performance of *yajña*s such as the *aśvamedha*, and this encouraged the search for the sites of the rituals.[55] Two structures were interpreted as altars, but recent opinion has rejected such interpretations.[56] Had there been any fire altars in the vicinity of the city, it is most likely that they would have been discovered, since the original location of Nagarjunakonda at a lower elevation in the valley was carefully and systematically explored, the excavation being part of a project of 'salvage archeology' carried out before the site was submerged on completion of the Tungabhadra dam.

By the early centuries AD the Vedic sacrificial rituals, inasmuch as they were performed by monarchs, appear to have acquired another dimension. They became a legitimizing ritual for kings, particularly for those seeking connections with the two royal lineages of *kṣatriya* ancestry, the Sūryavaṃśa and the Candravaṃśa. This may also in part explain the bifurcation of royal patronage to religious sects, where the women of the royal families – as, for example, the Ikṣvākus – were equally zealous in their support of Buddhism, which support is amply reflected in the monuments and inscriptions of the time.

The one site that can be described without hesitation as that of a fire altar is at Jagatgram.[57] It was discovered in the course of exploration in the Dehra Dun district where the Yamuna River descends from the Siwalik hills to the plains. It lies in the vicinity of Kalsi, better known as the site of a series of rock edicts of the Mauryan emperor Aśoka. Three sites were exposed where a king had performed *aśvamedhas*. Each site consisted of an eagle-shaped altar. Inscribed bricks from the first site provide the information that a king, Śīlavarmaṇa, performed four *aśvamedhas* at Jagatgram. One inscription reads:

> *siddham aum yugeśvarasyāśvamedhe yugaśailamahipate iṣṭakā vārṣaganasya nṛpateśīlavarmaṇa*
>
> 'Hail! Brick from the altar of the *aśvamedha* of the king Śīlavarmaṇa of the Varṣagana, the lord of Yugaśaila, the Yugeśvara.'

Another brick inscription reads:

> *nṛpatervarṣaganasya poṇaṣaṣṭhasya dhīmata caturatthasyāśva medhasya citoyam Śīlavarmaṇa*
>
> 'Altars of the four aśvamedhas of the renowned king Śīlavarmaṇa of the Varṣagana, sixth in descent from Poṇa.'

It has been suggested that the Varṣagana-gotra may be the same as that referred to by Pāṇini as the sixty-ninth *gotra*, Vṛṣagana,[58] and the word *yugeśvara* suggests 'the lord of the lustrum' described in the *Bṛhat Saṃhitā*. The latter might indicate that the repeated performance of the ceremony had to do with the purification of the king or the people. The identity of Śīlavarmaṇa remains obscure, as also does his line of descent from Poṇa. He may have been associated with the rulers of Lakha-maṇḍala in this area. Paleographically the inscription written in Brāhmī dates to the third century AD. The bricks bearing the inscription are of two sizes, 1:2:3 and 1:2:4. The area obviously had settlements during the Mauryan period for there to have been a set of edicts inscribed nearby. Excavations in the neighborhood indicate more evolved settlements dating to the start of the Christian era.[59]

The *agnicayana* altar as a structure is proceeded with, layer by layer, and in a sense the same pattern of construction may have gone into the ultimate form of the ritual. Archaeologically there is no clearly defined culture or period to which it can be related. The pottery-making techniques suggest Neolithic practices, the forms of the pottery carry traces of Chalcolithic types, the bricks are strongly reminiscent of a Harappan urban culture, the hawk shape of the altar echoes shamanistic ideas, and the inclusion of both human and animal bones suggests analogies with Megalithic funerary monuments. The increasing emphasis on a form of pot-latch included within the rites points to a people probably no longer nomadic and with enough wealth to be distributed and consumed on a ritual occasion. The *agnicayana* ritual was gradually put together, modified, adjusted, and elaborated upon in the course of centuries. It was likely to have been extended by additional rites, taken perhaps from a variety of cultures, but the additions were interlocked in a vast edifice of ritual. In this process its purpose and function also underwent change. Beginning as a ritual performed for the acquisition of magical power linked to the concept of an immortal self and for the expression of communion between men and gods, it incorporated in its development notions of fertility, wealth, and power, and emerged as a ritual of legitimation and social validation. Its very survival into the present takes on yet another dimension, the historical dimension, that is different from those with which it started.

References

1. A clear case of transhumance being tied into trade is that of the sheep and yak herders along the Himalayan borders who became the backbone of what has been called a 'vertical economy' – in this case, between Tibet and India.
2. M. Rowton, 'Enclosed Nomadism', *JESHO*, 17, 1974, pp. 1–30.
3. ṚV, 7.96.2; 7.8.4; 7.18.3.

4. Rene Labat, 'Elam and Western Persia, c. 1200–1000 BC', in *Cambridge Ancient History*, II.2, p. 506.

5. A. Goetze, 'The Struggle for the Domination of Syria (1400–1300 BC)', in *Cambridge Ancient History*, II.2, pp. 1–8, 109-10.

5. Iron occurs at sites in central India and the Ganga-Yamuna Doāb by the end of the second millennium BC although recently earlier dates have been suggested. At sites in the Gandhāra Grave Culture it occurs at the start of the first millennium BC. It is earlier in Megalithic sites in the peninsula. After the eighth century BC it becomes more noticeable. If it was one of the technological levers in the acceptance of Indo-Aryan, then it might have been appropriated in the north by speakers of Indo-Aryan. Its use in the peninsula would then have had an independent entry, since most scholars tend to identify the Megalithic builders with Dravidian speakers (B. K. Gururaja Rao, pp. 330ff). For a discussion on iron, see D. Chakrabarti, 'The Beginning of Iron in India', *Antiquity*, 50, 1976, pp. 114–24.

7. ṚV, 1.162, 1.163.

8. KŚS, 20.1; ASS, 10.6.1ff.

9. *Mahābhārata*, 14.90.

10. *Rāmāyaṇa*, 1.12-13

11. B. K. Thapar, 'Kalibangan: A Harappan Metropolis Beyond the Indus Valley', *Expedition*, Winter, 1975, pp. 19–32. Cf. *Agni*, vol. I, p. 154.

12. Th. Bloch, 'Excavation at Lauriya', *Annual Report of the Archaeological Survey of India*: 1905,1906, pp. 11–15; W. Caland, *De Archaeologische vondsten in de heuvels van Lauriya*, Amsterdam, 1912. I am grateful to Professor Staal for drawing my attention to this discussion, and for translating Caland's paper for me.

13. A point that incidentally seems to be contradicted in the ŚB, 13.8.1.5, refers to the *devas* making their burial places four-cornered, whereas the Asuras, Prācyas, and others make them round.

14. ŚB, 2.5.1.3; *Sacred Books of the East*, XII, p. 385.

15. *History of Dharmaśāstra*, IV, pp. 246ff, n. 559; ŚB, 13.8.1–4; KŚS, 28.4.4. A. Parpola, *South Indian Megaliths*, Madras, 1973, pp. 30ff. Professor Staal informs me that there is a rather vague tradition among the Nambudiris that in the past some had the practice of the

yajamāna or his wife (whoever died first) being cremated on his *agnicayana* altar.

16. V. R. Ramachandra Dikshitar, 'Origins and Early History of the Caityas', *Indian Historical Quarterly*, 14, 1938, pp. 440–51.

17. *Majjhima Nikāya*, I.20; *Jātaka*, I.237; VI.173; *Dhammapada*, 188.

18. *Borobudur*, Paris, 1935.

19. 1.12.1–4.

20. *Mahābhārata*, 1.102.12; 6.3.37. *Rāmāyaṇa*, 5.10.15.

21. *Rāmāyaṇa*, 5.41.10ff.

22. TS, 5.4.11; KŚS, 16.5.9. Also BŚS, 17.29, below, pp. 668–71.

23. B. Rowland, *The Art and Architecture of India*, Harmondsworth, Eng., 1959, p. 254.

24. J. Bloch, *Les Inscriptions d'Aśoka*, Paris, 1950, p. 158.

25. The references appear to be to the piling up of wood, ṚV, 1.112.17; 1.158.4.

26. P. C. Pant, 'Megaliths of Jangal Mahal and Vedic Tradition', paper read at Post-Conference Session at Deccan College, Poona, Dec. 1978. See also *Indian Archaeology—A Review*, 1963-64, pp. 40-1.

27. As for example among the Khasi tribes of Meghalaya and other parts of north-eastern India, where this tradition has continued up to recent times.

28. The details regarding the bricks have been discussed in F. Staal (ed.), *Agni*, Vol. I.

29. H. S. Converse, 'The *Agnicayana* Rite: Indigenous Origin?', *History of Religion*, 14.2, 1974, pp. 81–95.

30. Ibid., p. 83.

31. Ibid., p. 84.

32. S. Piggott, pp. 273ff.

33. ŚB, 6.5.4; BSS, 10.1–8.

34. ŚB, 14.1.2; C. G. Kashikar, 'Pottery in Vedic Literature', *Indian Journal of the History of Science*, 4.1-2, 1969, pp. 15–26; W. Rau, 'Vedic Texts on the Manufacture of Pottery', *Journal of the Oriental*

Institute, Baroda, 23.3, 1974, pp. 137–42; Y. Ikari, below, pp. 168–77.

35. ŚB, 6.5.4.4; 14.1.2.21; KSS, 16.4.11.

36. ŚB, 14.1.2.17; BSS, 9.4.

37. BŚS, 11.1–4.

38. BŚS, 10.1–8.

39. BŚS, 11.1–4; Kashikar, p. 20.

40. MS, 1.8.3.

41. For some of this information on potting techniques and the firing of pottery, I am grateful to a modern potter, Gouri Khosla, with whom I discussed the details given in the texts.

42. Henry Hodges, *Artefacts*, London, 1964, pp. 20ff.

43. R. Mughal, 'Explorations in Northern Baluchistan, 1972: New Evidence and Fresh Interpretations', *Proceedings of the Second Annual Symposium on Archaeological Research in Iran*, 1973, p. 278.

44. Kashikar, p. 26 n. 23; R. S. Panchmukhi, *Progress of Kannada Research in Bombay Province from 1941–46*, Dharwar, 1948, I-II; pp. 2.63-5.

45. Converse, op.cit.; Kashikar, op.cit.; Rau, op.cit.

46. Kashikar, p. 20.

47. ĀŚS, 15.3.20, quoted in Eggeling, *Sacred Books of the East*, XLIV, p. 456 n. 3.

48. 4.17.4; 5.31.1.

49. ŚB, 6.6.2.6; VS, 11.69; TS, 4.1.9.

50. ṚV, 3.53.7; 10.67.2. Cf. *Agni*, Vol. I, pp. 138, 162.

51. Kashikar, op. cit.

52. G. R. Sharma, *The Excavation at Kausambi* (1957–59), Allahabad, 19 60, pp. 87ff.

53. *Kandahāla Jātaka*, no. 542.

54. G. R. Sharma, Plate 31B, Fig. 18.4 facing p. 89; Plate 32A, Fig. 18.1 facing p. 89.

55. T. N. Ramachandran, *Nagarjunakonda*, Calcutta, 1938. M.A.S.I. No. 71 .

56. H. Sarkar and B. N. Misra, *Nagarjunakonda*, New Delhi, 1972, p. 20.

57. *Indian Archaeology—A Review* (1953-54), pp. 10-11; T. N. Ramachandran, 'Aśvamedha Site near Kalsi', *Journal of Oriental Research*, 21, 1953, pp. 1–31.

58. Pāṇini, 4.1.105.

59. N. C. Ghosh and R. P. Sharma, 'The Cultures of the Early Historical Period in the Siwalik Ranges Between Ganga and Yamuna', paper presented at the Archaeological Society Conference, Chandigarh, 1975.

Index

ādivāsī 38, 69
Afghanistan 15, 82, 107, 125, 126, 127, 129, 131, 141, 144, 145, 162
Agni vi, 23, 50, 63, 91, 107, 140, 141, 142, 146, 149, 183, 184, 185
Ahura Mazda 50, 54, 127, 132, 136
Aitareya Brāhmaṇa 58, 116, 117, 118, 158
Ājīvikas 59, 116
Anatolia 3, 8, 16, 46, 49, 52, 54, 57, 126
Aṅga 97, 114
Arabian peninsula 7
Araṭṭa 132
Archaeology 1, 2, 3, 7, 8, 18, 45, 46, 52, 55, 78, 81, 82, 127, 156, 161
Arthaśāstra 117
Arya Samaj 13, 40, 41
āryavarta 71
Aśoka Maurya 116, 169, 181, 184
astronomy 51, 95, 96, 104, 112
Āśvalāyana Gṛhyasūtra 168
Atharvaveda 9, 26, 92, 110, 111, 113, 114, 116, 117, 134
Aurobindo 13, 44
Avesta 3, 4, 8, 17, 30, 49, 50, 51, 52, 54, 55, 57, 61, 126, 127, 130, 131, 132, 135, 136, 138, 144

Bactria 127, 130
Bactro-Margiana Archaeological Complex 53, 127, 130
Balbūtha 140, 145, 146
Baluchistan 7, 8, 16, 47, 54, 78, 90, 107, 185
Baudhāyana Dharma Sūtra 114, 117
Besant, Annie 71
Bharata 131, 132, 141, 142
Bhaviṣya Purāṇa 118
bilingualism 16, 17, 53, 82, 151, 163
Blavatsky, Madame 13, 41
Bopp, F. 30
Brāhmaṇas 85, 141
Buddhaghoṣa 108
Burnouf, E. 30